802.11ac: A Survival Guide

Matthew S. Gast

Beijing · Cambridge · Farnham · Köln · Sebastopol · Tokyo

802.11ac: A Survival Guide

by Matthew S. Gast

Printed in the United States of America.

Published by O'Reilly Media, Inc., 1005 Gravenstein Highway North, Sebastopol, CA 95472.

O'Reilly books may be purchased for educational, business, or sales promotional use. Online editions are also available for most titles (*http://safaribooksonline.com*). For more information, contact our corporate/institutional sales department: 800-998-9938 or *corporate@oreilly.com*.

Editors: Mike Loukides and Meghan Blanchette	**Cover Designer:** Karen Montgomery
Production Editor: Kristen Borg	**Interior Designer:** David Futato
Proofreader: Rachel Head	**Illustrators:** Robert Romano and Rebecca Demarest

August 2013:   First Edition

Revision History for the First Edition:

2013-07-22:   First release

2015-07-17:   Second release

See *http://oreilly.com/catalog/errata.csp?isbn=9781449343149* for release details.

ISBN: 978-1-449-34314-9

[LSI]

For L.,

who reminds me it's okay to have my head in the clouds sometimes.

And for the NCSA instruction team who made me into a pilot so I can get there:

Mike, Terence, Larry, Mike, John, Buzz, and John.

Table of Contents

Foreword

Today, it's easy to take Wi-Fi and its magical benefits for granted. Wi-Fi is a fundamental part of our Internet ecosystem—it's hard to imagine a world without it. In fact, the world without Wi-Fi wouldn't be the world we have; we'd be missing out on vast elements of the Internet's potential.

But the invention of Wi-Fi wasn't inevitable. The technological innovation we call Wi-Fi required a major innovation in U.S. government spectrum policy.

Wi-Fi is a use of spectrum on an *unlicensed* basis, and the Federal Communications Commission (the U.S. government agency created more than 75 years ago to manage communications, including those using electromagnetic spectrum) didn't allow that type of use until 1985. Spectrum frequencies were assigned only on an exclusive *licensed* basis. These exclusive licenses—granted to launch radio, TV, satellite, and backhaul transmissions—helped create tremendous economic and social value, so maybe it wasn't a surprise that the FCC hadn't authorized spectrum bands for unlicensed use.

But then, along came an idea: there were some bands of spectrum that were lying largely fallow—at 900 MHz, 2.4 GHz, and 5.8 GHz. Nobody could figure out what they could be licensed for. The bands were surrounded by other commercial uses, and transmissions at high or even moderate power levels or distances would cause interference. These became known as the "garbage" or "junk bands," and they sat there.

That is, until a brilliant policy innovator named Michael Marcus, an FCC staff engineer, suggested that this spectrum be made available for use *without* a license and on a shared basis, as long as the transmissions were at low power levels and they didn't interfere with neighboring licensed uses.

The bet was that innovators would figure out how to weave value out of that spectrum. Although it wasn't framed this way at the time, the idea was simple, forward-looking, and in retrospect, obviously consistent with the great arc of American invention: provide a platform for innovation, and innovators will come.

So on May 9, 1985, the FCC adopted a little-noticed Order on "spread spectrum technology" that opened up the junk bands. And innovators got to work.

Before long, someone had invented garage-door openers using unlicensed spectrum; then wireless microphones, cordless phones, Bluetooth, and eventually Wi-Fi.

Wi-Fi has had staggering success: from a standing start, it's now been adopted in roughly 200 million households worldwide. There are more than 750,000 Wi-Fi hot spots globally, and over 800 million Wi-Fi-enabled devices are sold every year. And all of these metrics are growing.

Devices and services built on unlicensed spectrum are an essential part of the U.S. economy: studies estimate that unlicensed spectrum generates as much as $37 billion annually for the U.S. economy. Wi-Fi hot spots in the United States increase the value of licensed broadband service by an estimated $25 billion a year.

And the benefits have dovetailed into other key sectors: 80% of wireless healthcare innovations, for example, are now on done on unlicensed spectrum, according to one report. Unlicensed spectrum is transforming our homes, with amazing products already in the market offering entirely new and exciting ways to enjoy music and video, and other products to drive energy efficiency. Wi-Fi is a key basis of machine-to-machine communications—or the Internet of Things—a swiftly emerging market with potential to transform any number of sectors; we've had a 300% increase in connected M2M devices using unlicensed spectrum in the past five years, and that's just the beginning.

In other words, unlicensed spectrum is a boon for the American economy, and it continues today to provide start-ups and innovators access to a test bed for spectrum that is used by millions, helping bring new technologies to consumers in a rapid fashion.

Wi-Fi hasn't been the only major spectrum policy innovation in the last three decades.

The FCC pioneered spectrum auctions for the world in the 1990s—an alternative to the less-efficient, case-by-case administration of licenses through lotteries and comparative hearings—and has since conducted over 80 auctions, granting more than 30,000 licenses. These auctions have generated over $50 billion for the U.S. Treasury and, even more important, over $500 billion in value for the U.S. economy, according to expert economists.

The FCC also, quite consequentially, began to grant spectrum licenses for *flexible* use, rather than strictly circumscribing use to particular purposes. Flexible spectrum rights help ensure spectrum moves to uses valued most highly by markets and consumers, and the FCC has been hard at work the past few years to maximize flexibility and remove outdated use rules and restrictions.

Together, licensed and unlicensed spectrum have given us the amazing mobile Internet ecosystem we enjoy today—smartphones, tablets, the new "apps economy," and more. And the mobile revolution is driving economic growth, job creation, and U.S. competitiveness. Nearly $250 billion in private capital has been invested in U.S. wired and wireless broadband networks since 2009; there's been more private investment in ICT than any other U.S. sector, including by major oil and gas or auto companies. The U.S. is the first country deploying 4G LTE networks at scale, and in late 2012 we had as many LTE subscribers as the rest of the world combined, making us the global test bed for next generation 4G apps and services.

The new mobile apps economy—a made-in-the-U.S.A. phenomenon—has already created more than 500,000 U.S. jobs, and more than 90% of smartphones sold globally in 2012 run operating systems developed by U.S. companies, up from 25% three years ago. Annual investment in U.S. wireless networks grew more than 40% between 2009 and 2012, while investment in European wireless networks was flat, and wireless investment in Asia—including China—was up only 4%.

But we know we face big challenges to our mobile momentum. None is greater than the spectrum crunch.

Spectrum is a limited resource. Yet smartphones and tablets are being adopted faster than any communications or computing device in history; U.S. mobile data traffic grew almost 300% last year, and is projected to grow an additional 16-fold by 2016. Wi-Fi and other unlicensed innovations are key to bridging this supply/demand gap. Wi-Fi already carries more Internet traffic than cellular networks, and commercial mobile carriers are offloading 33% of all traffic to Wi-Fi, with that amount projected to grow to 46% by 2017.

So with the U.S. mobile ecosystem booming and demand for spectrum skyrocketing, policymakers need to free up a large amount of new spectrum for both licensed and unlicensed use.

Fortunately, the FCC has been focused on this task. Early in the Obama administration, the FCC released the country's first National Broadband Plan, which included a goal of freeing up 300 MHz of spectrum (including both licensed and unlicensed) by 2015 and 500 MHz by 2020, essentially doubling the amount of airwaves available for broadband by decade's end. We will achieve the 2015 goal, and with continued focus and leadership, we can achieve the 2020 goal as well.

In 2010, the FCC freed up the largest amount of low-band spectrum for unlicensed use in 25 years by making high-quality "white spaces" spectrum available in between TV channels. And in early 2013, the FCC passed a plan to increase unlicensed spectrum for Wi-Fi by about 35%—unleashing 195 MHz in the 5 GHz band.

But we need more—more spectrum and more policy innovation.

Incentive auctions are one such major next-generation spectrum policy innovation. Proposed in 2010 as part of the National Broadband Plan, incentive auctions are two-sided and use the power of the market to repurpose beachfront spectrum used by TV broadcasters (in the 600 MHz band) for both licensed and unlicensed wireless broadband. In 2012, Congress passed and President Obama signed landmark legislation authorizing the auctions; the FCC is on track to hold the world's first incentive auction in 2014.

In addition to freeing up a large amount of spectrum for licensed use, incentive auctions have the potential to unleash a next-generation of unlicensed spectrum. So, as part of the auction, the FCC proposed setting aside a significant amount of the returned broadcast spectrum for unlicensed use. To my surprise, this has been met with some opposition. Some say 100% of the recovered spectrum should be auctioned for exclusive licensed use. This would be a mistake, as it shuts down a potential new opportunity for innovation. And as Matthew Gast and others have demonstrated, if we build new platforms for innovation, the innovators will come.

Meanwhile, innovators continue to make tremendous strides around existing unlicensed spectrum, particularly Wi-Fi. Wi-Fi is making more efficient use of spectrum, with incredible boosts in speed, capacity, and reliability. I'm confident the new 802.11ac standard for Gigabit Wi-Fi—and Matthew Gast's important guide—will demonstrate anew the powerful value of the unlicensed platform.

For years, Matthew Gast has worked tirelessly to unleash the opportunities of Wi-Fi. This book is another significant contribution to the future of Wi-Fi and the mobile Internet. And it comes at just the right time.

—Julius Genachowski

Julius Genachowski served as Chairman of the U.S. Federal Communications Commission from June 2009 to May 2013.

Preface

People keep moving. Networks still don't, but they are being forced—sometimes quite painfully!—to accommodate the motion of users.

Wireless LANs are well established as The Way to Connect to the Network. When I first moved to Silicon Valley in the late 1990s, it was common to hear people talk about how they had run Ethernet through their homes so that every room had a network jack. Friends of mine worked with their home builders to install their own wiring, and occasionally a renovated home's listing would breathlessly tout network connectivity. (To those who knew the technology, networking was always more than a patch panel installed someplace convenient.)

Today, network wiring no longer has a monopoly on that initial connection to the network edge. From Ethernet, the world has shifted to using wireless LANs, almost exclusively based on the 802.11 family of standards. In the space of a decade, Ethernet has been transformed from the underlying technology that made jokes like "will code for Internet access" possible into a mere support system for the wireless network that everybody attaches to.

The road to becoming the "first hop" technology in the network has required several steps. When 802.11 was first standardized in 1997, many of the networks ran at just one megabit, with a really fast network (for that point in time) running at double that speed. At that time, there was a huge debate between the proponents of frequency hopping technology and direct sequence technology. Direct sequence won out and led to the first mainstream technology, 802.11b. The wireless network community would move from a single radio carrier to multi-carrier technology with 802.11a and 802.11g, and on to multiple-input/multiple-output (MIMO) with 802.11n.

The next big milestone for 802.11 is a speed that is, as Dogbert would say, "big and round"[1]—a gigabit per second of raw speed. That project is currently in development as 802.11ac. If you wished 802.11n were faster, buckle up and start reading!

Audience

This book is about 802.11ac, the draft standard "gigabit WiFi" specification. After the massive revision that was 802.11n, the technology changes in 802.11ac are (fortunately) not quite as large. To get the most out of this book, you'll need to be familiar with the basics of the 802.11 Medium Access Control (MAC) layer, and have some familiarity with how pre-802.11ac networks were designed and built.

 Think of this book as the 802.11ac-specific companion to the earlier *802.11 Wireless Networks: The Definitive Guide* from 2005, and *802.11n: A Survival Guide*, published in 2012.

The intended reader is a network professional who needs to get in-depth information about the technical aspects of 802.11ac network operations, deployment, and monitoring. Readers in positions such as the following will benefit the most from this book:

- Network architects responsible for the design of the wireless networks at their places of business, whether the 802.11ac network is the first wireless LAN or an upgrade from a previous 802.11 standard

- Network administrators responsible for building or maintaining an 802.11ac network, especially those who want to make the transition from earlier 802.11a/b/g or 802.11n technologies

If you have picked up this book looking for information on security in 802.11ac, it's in here. Fortunately, 802.11ac is just as secure as previous generations of 802.11. Security is part of the protocol, so if you are comfortable with 802.11 security in 802.11n or earlier, you know everything you need to know about 802.11ac.

Conventions Used in This Book

The following typographical conventions are used in this book:

Italic
Indicates new terms, URLs, email addresses, filenames, and file extensions.

---

1. As always, Dogbert was ahead of the curve. He was frightening people way back in 1994 (*http://dilbert.com/strips/comic/1994-03-24/*).

This icon signifies a tip, suggestion, or general note.

This icon indicates a warning or caution.

Safari® Books Online

Safari Books Online (*www.safaribooksonline.com*) is an on-demand digital library that delivers expert content in both book and video form from the world's leading authors in technology and business.

Technology professionals, software developers, web designers, and business and creative professionals use Safari Books Online as their primary resource for research, problem solving, learning, and certification training.

Safari Books Online offers a range of product mixes and pricing programs for organizations, government agencies, and individuals. Subscribers have access to thousands of books, training videos, and prepublication manuscripts in one fully searchable database from publishers like O'Reilly Media, Prentice Hall Professional, Addison-Wesley Professional, Microsoft Press, Sams, Que, Peachpit Press, Focal Press, Cisco Press, John Wiley & Sons, Syngress, Morgan Kaufmann, IBM Redbooks, Packt, Adobe Press, FT Press, Apress, Manning, New Riders, McGraw-Hill, Jones & Bartlett, Course Technology, and dozens more. For more information about Safari Books Online, please visit us online.

How to Contact Us

Please address comments and questions concerning this book to the publisher:

O'Reilly Media, Inc.
1005 Gravenstein Highway North
Sebastopol, CA 95472
800-998-9938 (in the United States or Canada)
707-829-0515 (international or local)
707-829-0104 (fax)

We have a web page for this book, where we list errata, examples, and any additional information. You can access this page at *http://oreil.ly/80211ac_guide*.

To comment or ask technical questions about this book, send email to *bookques tions@oreilly.com*.

For more information about our books, courses, conferences, and news, see our website at *http://www.oreilly.com*.

Find us on Facebook: *http://facebook.com/oreilly*

Follow us on Twitter: *http://twitter.com/oreillymedia*

Watch us on YouTube: *http://www.youtube.com/oreillymedia*

Acknowledgments

This is my second book written with Meg Blanchette as editor. Meg kept the book moving along as best she could, which is no small feat given that I successfully pursued a pilot cetificate as I wrote this book. Meg regularly sought out opportunities for me to experiment as an author, most notably by encouraging me to participate in the early release program starting six months before the book's final release. All the delays in publication are due entirely to my preoccupation with aviation, and would no doubt have been much worse without Meg's diligent efforts to keep me on track.

I could not have asked for better readers to keep me motivated. As a direct result of all the notes and questions that I received, the book grew substantially during the review cycle. The review team included several 802.11 luminaries who are famous in their own right. My all-star review team consisted of (in alphabetical order, so I do not need to try and rank their many valuable and varied contributions in any sort of order):

Joe Fraher
> Joe is a technical writer and colleague of mine at Aerohive, where he consistently produces documentation that is lucid, complete, and easy to use. Unlike me, he has mastered all the tools of his trade and handles the whole project from start to finish. One of Joe's main contributions to the finished product you now hold is that he does not let me get away with glossing over anything. If you find that the book is consistent and complete, your thanks are properly given to Joe.

Changming Liu
> Changming is the CTO at Aerohive, and a fountain of ideas both for Aerohive's customers, and for me personally. I cannot name a conversation with him that I did not wish were longer.

Chris Lyttle
> Chris heads up the wireless LAN practice at a major integrator, where he helps customers figure out how to use the technology that we build as an industry. Along

the way, he chronicles the journey on his blog at Wi-Fi Kiwi (*http://www.wifiki wi.com*), sharing valuable bits of information with anybody who is trying to run a wireless LAN.

Craig Mathias

At the Farpoint Group, Craig has been a prolific writer on 802.11 for many years. I am indebted to him for his many kind words over the years, and the encouragement he has always given me to continue writing on 802.11. Craig has asked me to be on many panels at industry events over the years, and has never failed to promote my books in his thoughtful introductions. As an analyst on the cutting edge, Craig is able to talk about new developments throughout the development process.

Matthew Norwood

Matthew, a senior technologist at an integrator, is one of the many people in the industry who has to do useful things with the crazy collection of technology parts we create. His networking mad science, which is about many components in addition to wireless LANs, unfolds at In Search of Tech (*http://www.insearchof tech.com/*).[2] Matthew brought the sensibility of an expert network engineer to the book, and his review of the planning and integration parts of this book was particularly valuable.

Adrian Stephens

Adrian is one of the leaders of the 802.11 working group, where he has consistently used computers to save work instead of creating more of it. Talking to Adrian is like dropping questions into a deep well of technical knowledge. (For the record, I have yet to find the bottom.) I benefited from Adrian's prodigious knowledge when we worked together on the 802.11-2012 revision, and he continues to serve the 802.11 community in ways too numerous to count. His comments on advanced MAC features and beamforming particularly strengthened the text, and his humourous[3] comments added levity to the long slog of finishing the book, the effect of which was to help me see the light at the end of the tunnel.

Tim Zimmerman

Tim is an analyst with a technology advisory firm, and one of the most plugged-in people in the Wi-Fi industry. I am grateful for his time, and his many comments expanded multiple parts of the book in ways that will benefit you.

---

2. Matthew also wrote the nicest thing I've ever read about my writing on his own blog at *http://www.insearch oftech.com/2013/04/11/the-curse-of-matthews-books/*.

3. Adrian is English, so I deviate from the American spelling just to show him that I can be bilingual.

In addition to the formal review team, I benefited from the assistance of many other readers. Early release readers came from all across the world. Some of the most helpful were:

Jeff Haydel

> Jeff is a talented field engineer for Aerohive, and was all that an author could ask for in an early release reader. He religiously read multiple drafts of the book, and was particularly helpful in striking the right balance between remaining faithful to the specification while trying to be concise and comprehensible.

Colleen Szymanik

> Colleen Szymanik runs one of the largest and most complex wireless networks in the world, and her comments kept me focused on how to keep the book focused on information that would help working network administrators everywhere.

Ben Wilson

> My colleague Ben Wilson has helped deploy more wireless networks than I care to count. His work takes him all across the UK, and I cannot figure out how he found time to review the book, let alone offer numerous useful suggestions.

One of the advantages of publishing the book early was that readers were able to interact with each other, both in person and on blogs. As I was working on incorporating technical review comments, I finally met Lee Badman face-to-face at Interop, and our brief discussion was critical to refining my thinking about the connectivity that will support future generations of 802.11ac access points.

I am grateful to readers who served as valuable sanity checks during the writing process, and helped keep me as focused as possible on the end goal. Terry Simons, who works on wireless LAN integration for Nest Labs, found the time to review the draft of this book and give me the detailed technical feedback of somebody who knows what it takes to make Wi-Fi just work. Tom Hollingsworth offered encouragement at a critical juncture. Michele Chubirka, the security podcaster for Packet Pushers, provided a much-welcomed reality check during the middle of the long twilight of the book. Kelly Davis-Felner and Bill Solominsky at the Wi-Fi Alliance offered encouragement both in person at the Wi-Fi Alliance meeting where much of this book was written, and by drafting me into writing for the Wi-Fi Alliance on 802.11ac.

CHAPTER 1

Introduction to 802.11ac

> *If the network drops below a speed of five hundred*
> *megabits per second, the users will explode!*
>
> —The plot of the movie *Speed* (starring Keanu
> Reeves as a network administrator)

One of the many experiences I value from my time participating in the 802.11 working group is the ability to compare the "outside" view of a technology with the "inside" view of people in the engine room sweating to make it work. From the outside, wireless LANs have seen a steady progression in speeds from a megabit in the late 1990s to a gigabit with the first release of 802.11ac in 2013. Getting inside the process of making that happen let me see the false starts and wrong turns, and generally appreciate—and contribute to!—the behind-the-scenes work that creates that smooth external perception.

One important note about this book is that it is being written at the same time as the standard is being developed. It is possible that changes to 802.11ac will occur during the technical review process for the draft standard, though based on historical experience, I would expect any changes to be small at this point.

History

The 802.11 working group has a structured method of introducing new technologies. When a gap is identified in the existing standard, a sufficient number of participants can start a study group to investigate whether there is sufficient justification to develop new technology. Typically, as the Last Big Thing is wrapping up, the project to develop the Next Big Thing will begin. The structured method of developing new standards has led to a long history of innovation, delivering both new physical layers and enhancements to the Medium Access Control (MAC) layer in terms of security and quality of service, as shown in Figure 1-1.

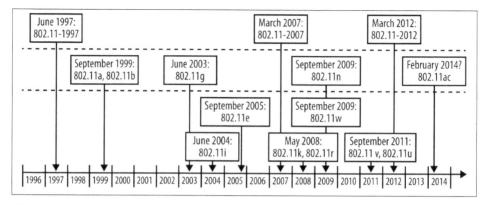

Figure 1-1. 802.11 timeline

In 2007, the 802.11n project was well underway, with a draft standard that was technically complete enough to enable multi-vendor interoperability. In May of that year, the
802.11 working group started the Very High Throughput (VHT) study group to launch
a project to create even faster networking. The VHT study group was chartered to
develop speeds in excess of 802.11n's 600 Mbps, and the genesis of 802.11ac dates to the
start of that study effort.

Once started, a study group works to propose to the IEEE as a whole to take on the
project in a document known as the Project Authorization Request (PAR). Part of the
PAR is to demonstrate that five key criteria are met, and if the criteria are not met, the
project does not move forward. They are:

- Broad market potential
- Compatibility
- Distinct identity
- Technical feasibility
- Economic feasibility

The VHT study group began its work at the May 2007 meeting, and it recommended
forming two gigabit networking task groups. The distinction between the two task
groups is the supported frequency band they operate in. Task Group AC was authorized
to build a gigabit standard that was supported at frequencies of less than 6 GHz, which
makes it compatible with the existing frequency bands used by 802.11. (Early in the
development process, it was decided to restrict 802.11ac to the 5 GHz frequency bands
used by 802.11n and 802.11a, and not to support the 2.4 GHz frequency band used by
802.11b and 802.11g.) Task Group AD was authorized to build a gigabit standard in a
frequency band around 60 GHz. While it is interesting technology, it requires significant

changes to the way that networks are planned and built, and the range is dramatically shorter with such a high frequency.

Once Task Group AC was authorized in September 2008, it began working on technical approaches to meet the goals laid out in its PAR.[1] The group was chartered in its PAR to produce a standard operating at 1 Gbps for multiple stations, and 500 Mbps for a single station which hints at some of the technical approaches that will be used to get to much higher speeds. Before starting work on writing the detailed technical specification, the task group approved a specification framework document. Beginning with a specification framework represented a departure from the 802.11 working group's typical practice of beginning with detailed technical proposals. By starting with a list of attributes for the final standard, Task Group AC was able to shorten the standards development process and move the technology to market more quickly.[2] Even though the 802.11ac PAR set out the goal of gigabit networking, that relatively modest goal will be met with first-generation products, and the full standard provides additional opportunities for significant additional speed gains.

802.11ac and 802.11ad: What Difference a Frequency Makes

Both the 802.11ac and 802.11ad efforts sprang out of the VHT study group. The standards effort for 802.11ad completed in late December 2012, shortly after this book went into early release. Although the standards effort for 802.11ac is ongoing, pre-release hardware for 802.11ac has been in development for a longer period of time and commercial products based on the draft standard are readily available. The major difference between the two that drives most comparisons is the operating frequency. 802.11ac was founded as gigabit at less than 6 GHz, which, practically speaking, keeps it constrained to the existing unlicensed frequency bands used by 802.11. 802.11ad started off in recognition of new spectrum available at 60 GHz in the US, Europe, and Japan. 802.11ad uses a very wide (4 GHz) channel and tops out with a conservative modulation (16-QAM) because the range of such high frequencies is typically short. With an intended short range, the 802.11ad specification changes the way that some fundamental operations of 802.11 occur so that it is more of a peer-to-peer protocol. Key applications for 802.11ad are the support of wireless docking and high-speed short-range cable replacement.

---

1. The final approved 802.11ac PAR is available at *https://mentor.ieee.org/802.11/dcn/08/11-08-0807-04-0vht-below-6-ghz-par-nescom-form-plus-5cs.doc*.

2. The specification framework document is 11-09/0992, which was at revision 21 as of this book's writing. The most recent version of the specification framework can be downloaded from *https://mentor.ieee.org/802.11/documents?is_dcn=992&is_group=00ac&is_year=2009*.

The Core Technology of 802.11ac

At first glance, 802.11ac appears to be an exercise intended to make Claude Shannon nervous by packing more bits into each slice of spectrum and time.[3] Conceptually, 802.11ac is an evolution from 802.11n and not a revolutionary departure. Many of the techniques used to increase speed in 802.11ac are familiar after the introduction of MIMO. Unlike 802.11n, which developed major new MAC features to improve efficiency, 802.11ac uses familiar techniques and takes them to a new level, with one exception. Rather than using MIMO only to increase the number of data streams sent to a single client, 802.11ac is pioneering a multi-user form of MIMO that enables an access point (AP) to send to multiple clients at the same time. Table 1-1 lays out the differences.

Table 1-1. Differences between 802.11n and 802.11ac

802.11n	802.11ac
Supports 20 and 40 MHz channels	Adds 80 and 160 MHz channels
Supports 2.4 GHz and 5 GHz frequency bands	Supports 5 GHz only
Supports BPSK, QPSK, 16-QAM, and 64-QAM	Adds 256-QAM
Supports many types of explicit beamforming	Supports only null data packet (NDP) explicit beamforming
Supports up to four spatial streams	Supports up to eight spatial streams (AP); client devices up to four spatial streams
Supports single-user transmission only	Adds multi-user transmission
Includes significant MAC enhancements (A-MSDU, A-MPDU)	Supports similar MAC enhancements, with extensions to accommodate high data rates

They include:

Wider channels

> 802.11ac introduces two new channel sizes: 80 MHz and 160 MHz. Just as with 802.11n, wider channels increase speed. In some areas, 160 MHz of contiguous spectrum will be hard to find, so 802.11ac introduces two forms of 160 MHz channels: a single 160 MHz block, and an "80+80 MHz" channel that combines two 80 MHz channels and gives the same capability.

256-QAM

> Like previous 802.11 amendments, 802.11ac transmits a series of symbols, each of which represents a bit pattern. Prior to 802.11ac, wireless LAN devices transmitted six bits in a symbol period. By using a more complex modulation that supports

---

3. In 1948, Shannon, then a Bell Labs researcher, developed the mathematical techniques to prove the maximum data speed that can be transmitted through a channel. The resulting "speed limit" of the channel is often called the *Shannon limit* or the *Shannon capacity*, and is related to both the signal-to-noise ratio of the channel and the channel's bandwidth. This is just one of his many important contributions that led to his title as "The Father of Information Theory."

more data bits, it is possible to send eight bits per symbol period, a gain of 30%. Details of QAM will be presented in Chapter 2. The extent to which 256-QAM can be used reliably in real-world deployments is an open question for 802.11ac at this time.

Beamforming

802.11ac radically simplifies the beamforming specifications to one preferred technical method. Beamforming in 802.11n required two devices to implement mutually agreeable beamforming functions from the available menu of options. Very few vendors implemented the same options, and as a result, there was almost no cross-vendor beamforming compatibility. With the key features of 802.11ac depending on beamforming, however, a simplification was required to enable the core technology.

More spatial streams and multi-user MIMO (MU-MIMO)

802.11ac specifies up to eight spatial streams, compared to 802.11n's four spatial streams, at the AP. The extra spatial streams can be used to transmit to multiple clients at the same time. With the ability to transmit at high speeds to multiple clients simultaneously, 802.11ac will speed up networks even more than might be apparent from simply looking at the data rate.

The Many Faces of Beamforming

Beamforming is a process by which the sender of a transmission can preferentially direct its energy toward a receiver to increase the signal-to-noise ratio, and hence the speed of the transmission. Broadly speaking, it can be grouped into two main types. *Explicit beamforming* is based on the transmitter and receiver exchanging information about the characteristics of the radio channel to extract maximum performance from the radio channel based on channel quality measurements, while *implicit beamforming* is based on inferences of channel characteristics when frames are lost. Explicit beamforming is generally more powerful because the channel measurements are more detailed than the inference of loss, but the explicit measurement and exchange of data on the radio link must be supported by both ends of the link. Transmitting beamformed frames typically requires an antenna array capable of altering its pattern on a frame-by-frame basis, which is why the term "smart antenna" is often used in discussions of beamforming. To change the radiation pattern on a frame-by-frame basis, smart antennas are controlled electronically.

Beamforming and Multi-User MIMO (MU-MIMO)

Multi-user MIMO represents the greatest potential of 802.11ac, though it has yet to be proven in commercially available products in widespread use. Prior to 802.11ac, all 802.11 standards were *single-user*: every transmission sent was sent to a single destination only. Beamforming is occasionally used in such networks as a means of increasing the signal power over a portion of the AP's territory to increase the data rate at the receiver. *Multi-user* transmissions are a new capability within 802.11. Radio waves, like any waves, add by superposition. If there are two receivers located in sufficiently different directions, a beamformed transmission may be sent to each of them at the same time.

Figure 1-2 compares the single-user MIMO technologies used in 802.11n with the new multi-user MIMO in 802.11ac. In Figure 1-2(a), all of the spatial streams are directed to one receiving device. In 2013, multiple spatial streams were a commonplace technical innovation, supported in every 802.11n AP and almost every client device. In contrast, Figure 1-2(b) shows what it means for a MIMO transmitter to be multi-user. In the figure, the access point is transmitting four simultaneous spatial streams. The magic of MU-MIMO is that the four spatial streams are being transmitted to three separate devices. Two of the spatial streams are transmitted to a laptop supporting high-speed data transmission. Each of the other two spatial streams is transmitted to a single-stream device, such as a phone or tablet computer. To keep the three transmissions separate, the AP uses beamforming to focus each of the transmissions toward its respective receiver. For this type of scenario to work, it is necessary that the receivers are located in different enough directions that focused transmissions avoid interfering with each other. Due to the potential of inter-stream interference, multi-user transmissions require more up-to-date feedback, a challenge that will be discussed more in Chapter 4.

Multi-user MIMO has the potential to change the way Wi-Fi networks are built because it enables better *spatial reuse*. One of the keys to building an 802.11 network of any type is reusing the same channel in multiple places. For example, in Figure 1-3(a), the radio channel is used for omnidirectional transmissions. When the AP transmits, the radio energy is received by both the laptop and the smartphone, and the channel may be used to communicate with only one of the devices at any point in time. One of the reasons why high-density networks are built on small coverage areas is that the same radio channel can be reused multiple times, and each AP in a dense network can transmit on the channel independently. Multi-user MIMO builds on the small-cell approach by enabling even more tightly packed networks. In Figure 1-3(b), MU-MIMO is in use. As a result, the AP can send independent transmissions within its own coverage area. Just as Ethernet switches reduced the collision domain from a whole broadcast segment to a single port, MU-MIMO reduces the spatial contention of a transmission and enables the first "switching-like" applications of Wi-Fi.

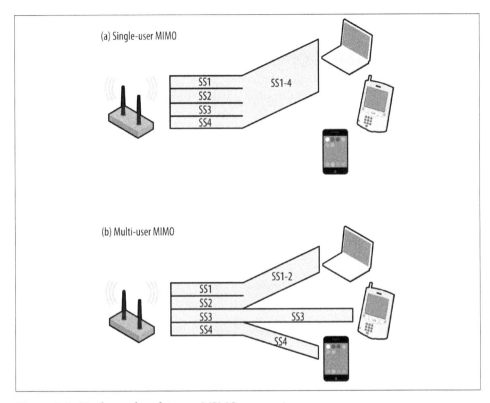

Figure 1-2. Single- and multi-user MIMO comparison

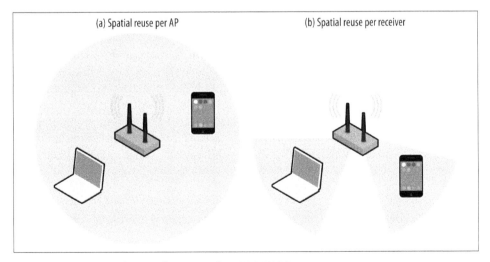

Figure 1-3. Improved spatial reuse with MU-MIMO

Getting MU-MIMO implementations right, however, is quite complex. The simple world of Figure 1-3 is an ideal depiction. In practice, there will always be some crosstalk between transmissions to different clients. As an implementation matter, each of the multiple transmissions in Figure 1-3(b) will be slower than the single transmission in Figure 1-3(a), but the total throughput in the multiple-transmission case will be larger.

Operating Frequency Band for 802.11ac

Unlike 802.11n, which operated all across the unlicensed spectrum bands allocated to wireless LANs, 802.11ac is restricted to 5 GHz operation only. 802.11ac's PAR stated that it would only work at 5 GHz. In effect, this is a recognition that 802.11n is as good as it's going to get for the 2.4 GHz band, and future technologies are not going to come to the old crowded spectrum there.

 802.11ac operates only in the 5 GHz frequency band. It is not available in the 2.4 GHz band.

Table 1-2 lists the 802.11 versions that operate in each frequency band.

Table 1-2. 802.11 standards operating in the 2.4 GHz and 5 GHz bands

2.4 GHz	5 GHz
802.11 (direct sequence and frequency hopping)	802.11a
802.11b	802.11n
802.11g	802.11ac
802.11n	

The decision to keep the 802.11ac specification from running in the 2.4 GHz band is frequently a source of questions from users who hope that 802.11ac will dramatically improve the performance of older 2.4 GHz devices. Unfortunately, there is sound technical justification for why 802.11n is the "end of the line" for the 2.4 GHz spectrum. Making 802.11n the capstone technology for the 2.4 GHz band is based on the relatively small benefit from the major features in 802.11ac. Most notably, one of the major techniques used to increase speed in 802.11ac is significantly wider channels. Doubling channel width to 40 MHz in 802.11n provided a little more than double the speed.

802.11ac goes even farther, to 80 and 160 MHz channels, but there is not 160 MHz of available spectrum to use in the old 2.4 GHz allocation.[4]

If, however, you decide to fully utilize the channel across the whole 80 MHz, by definition the entire open frequency band must be free of other transmissions. Using 40 MHz channels in a 2.4 GHz 802.11n network is hard enough because two of the three available transmission channels must be clear in order to transmit. Keeping all three 2.4 GHz channels clear would be even harder. If you can reliably keep all three available channels free, my only advice is to start buying lottery tickets because you clearly have luck with you. Even on a network that is intended only for use with new wide band 802.11ac devices, there will still be other narrowband devices. Too many battery-operated phones and tablets are in use to believe that a network can be restricted only to wide band devices.

The second big protocol feature to boost speed in 802.11ac is the move to the aggressive 256-QAM coding, which requires clean spectrum to have transmissions "land" on the right constellation point. (Don't worry, I'll write more about this in Chapter 2.) Spectrum at 5 GHz is much cleaner because there isn't interference from Bluetooth, microwave ovens, 2.4 GHz cordless phones, or any of the many random devices that pollute the 2.4 GHz band.[5] Although none of these devices taken alone does much to increase the noise level, taken together they may collectively raise the noise floor by about 5 dB overall. In some ways, regulation of 5 GHz operation is more protective, and tends to reduce interference as well. When you are trying to do something so channel quality–sensitive as 256-QAM, even small sources of noise are a major barrier.

802.11ac Product Development Plans

In the early days of 802.11, new physical layer specifications were smaller and came to market in one step. Starting with 802.11n, the technical specifications began to outrun product development capacity, and large specifications now come to the market in distinct waves. The first wave of 802.11ac products will be driven by the enthusiasm for higher speeds. APs will typically have three stream capabilities, but with 802.11ac providing 80 MHz channels and 256-QAM modulation, the speed will go from 450 Mbps to 1.3 Gbps. The second wave of 802.11ac products will add even wider channels and possibly even multi-user MIMO support, as outlined in Table 1-3. Later waves will add

---

4. The issue is actually a little more complicated. Most regulators require restrictions on side band emissions, so even if you have 83 MHz of spectrum, the harmonic lobes above and below the main 80 MHz transmission may be too powerful to meet side band emission requirements. When defining the channel width, 802.11ac has limits on the transmitted power outside the main band at ±120 MHz from the center frequency, and therefore, an 802.11ac channel does not fit in the 2.4 GHz band.

5. One reviewer pointed out to me that there have been some microwave ovens that operate around 5 GHz, but thankfully, they were not commercially successful.

even higher numbers of spatial streams and will usher in the multi-gigabit future promised by the 802.11ac project charter.

Table 1-3. Anticipated 802.11ac technology waves

Attribute	First wave	Second wave
Maximum number of spatial streams	3	3 or 4
Channel width	80 MHz	160 MHz
Maximum modulation	256-QAM	256-QAM
Typical maximum speed	1.3 Gbps	2.6 Gbps
Beamforming support	Varies (depending on vendor)	Yes
MU-MIMO support	No	Possibly

CHAPTER 2

The PHY

There's fifty-seven channels and no free airtime...
—Bruce Springsteen, singing "57 Channels
(And Nothin' On)" as a wireless administrator

Large improvements in 802.11 speeds typically have resulted from the introduction of a big new idea. Introducing multi-carrier transmission with OFDM increased speeds in the transition from 802.11b to 802.11a/g. Creating MIMO systems did the same in the move from 802.11a/g to 802.11n. 802.11ac, however, does not introduce a new way of transmitting data over the air. Though they are both extended beyond what was introduced in 802.11n, the techniques used to put bits on the air in 802.11ac will be familiar to anybody familiar with 802.11n: MIMO and wide channels. Raw speed increases in the PHY come from three sources: a higher number of MIMO streams, wider channels, and a finer modulation that can pack more bits into each unit of airtime.

Extended MIMO Operations

One of the major techniques used by 802.11ac to increase throughput is the extension of MIMO from a system that supports four spatial streams to one that supports eight. As with all other MIMO systems, each spatial stream requires its own transmission system; building an 802.11ac AP that supports eight spatial streams would therefore require an antenna array with eight independent radio chains and antennas. Taken as a single protocol feature, extending to eight spatial streams alone doubles throughput over an equivalent 802.11n system by doing something equivalent to doubling the number of lanes on a highway. It will, however, take time to bring devices with more than four spatial streams to market. Just as in previous versions of 802.11 MIMO systems, a transmitter must have at least one radio chain for transmission for each spatial stream; as devices support more spatial streams, the required antenna has more elements and will grow in size.

The number of spatial streams can be no greater than the number of elements in the antenna array. When the count of array elements exceeds the number of spatial streams, there is an additional signal processing gain that can be used to improve the signal-to-noise ratio in beamforming.

Beamforming is a capability that was first proposed in 802.11n, though it never achieved widespread implementation. By using the antenna array to send carefully phase-shifted energy patterns, it is possible to "steer" a data stream toward a particular receiver. 802.11ac builds on beamforming by allowing multiple simultaneous transmissions for multi-user MIMO (MU-MIMO). MU-MIMO is one of the key technologies that will take 802.11ac far beyond its published (or "headline") data rate for frame transmission. Instead of having a single transmitter and receiver in the same area, MU-MIMO enables *spatial reuse*, where the same channel can be used in different areas by the same access point. This exciting development will bring the benefits of switching and reduced collision domains to 802.11 networks. It is a topic that requires its own in-depth exposition because it requires communication between protocol layers; it is discussed fully in Chapter 4.[1]

Radio Channels in 802.11ac

To the well-established 20 MHz channel that has been widely used in 802.11 from the first standardization of OFDM in 802.11a and the 40 MHz channel used in 802.11n, the 802.11ac brings two new channel sizes. As expected, wider channels bring higher throughput. Just as in previous OFDM-based transmission, 802.11ac divides the channel into OFDM subcarriers, each of which has a bandwidth of 312.5 kHz. Each of the subcarriers is used as an independent transmission, and OFDM distributes the incoming data bits among the subcarriers. A few subcarriers are reserved and are called *pilot carriers*; they do not carry user data and instead are used to measure the channel.

Radio Channel Layout

To increase throughput, 802.11ac introduces two new channel widths. All 802.11ac devices are required to support 80 MHz channels, which doubles the size of the spectral channel over 802.11n. It further adds a 160 MHz channel option for even higher speeds. Due to the limitations of finding contiguous 160 MHz spectrum, the standard allows for a 160 MHz channel to be either a single contiguous block or two noncontiguous 80 MHz channels. Figure 2-1 shows the layout of channels in terms of their OFDM data

---

1. As you will see in Chapter 4, this is an (intentionally) simplified description of MIMO transmission. A single data stream does not necessarily follow a single clean, linear path through space, in large part due to the dependence of transmission on frequency.

and pilot carriers defined in 802.11ac, along with the channel formats from 802.11a/g and 802.11n for comparison. In the figure, each horizontal line represents the layout of OFDM subcarriers in one type of channel, ranging from the 20 MHz channels first used with OFDM up to the widest channel that 802.11ac has to offer. Pilot carriers are represented by the dips down in the line to show that they carry no data.

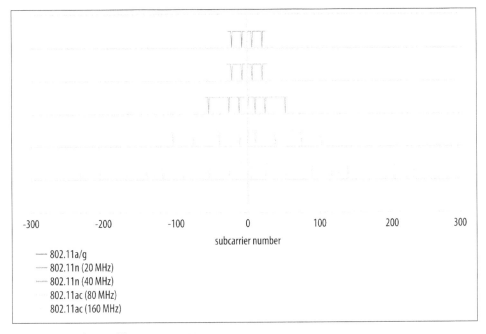

Figure 2-1. Channel layouts in 802.11ac

 This section describes the channel layout for a single 802.11ac radio. Most "802.11ac" APs that are sold initially will consist of a single 802.11ac 5 GHz radio plus a second 802.11n radio in the 2.4 GHz band.

Pilot carriers are a form of overhead used in OFDM, and they represent an overhead for the channel. In MIMO systems, a single pilot carrier can be more effective at assisting with the channel tuning operations. As a result, the pilot overhead in 802.11ac has almost a "bulk discount" effect with the wider channels. Table 2-1 identifies the OFDM carrier numbering and pilot channels. The range of the subcarriers defines the channel width itself. Each subcarrier has identical data-carrying capacity, and therefore, more is better. Pilot subcarriers are protocol overhead and are used to carry out important measurements of the channel. The table shows that as the channel size increases, the fraction of the channel devoted to pilot carriers decreases. As a result, the channel becomes more efficient as the width increases. The final two columns in the table depict the throughput relative to the capacity of two forms of 20 MHz channels in 802.11a/g and 802.11ac.

Table 2-1. Channel description attributes

PHY standard	Subcarrier range	Pilot subcarriers	Subcarriers (total/data)	Capacity relative to 802.11a/g	Capacity relative to 20 MHz 802.11ac
802.11a/g	−26 to −1, +1 to +26	±7, ±21	52 total, 48 usable (8% pilots)	x1.0	n/a
802.11n/ 802.11ac, 20 MHz	−28 to −1, +1 to +28	±7, ±21	56 total, 52 usable (7% pilots)	x1.1	x1.0
802.11n/ 802.11ac, 40 MHz	−58 to −2, +2 to +58	±11, ±25, ±53	114 total, 108 usable (5% pilots)	x2.3	x2.1
802.11ac, 80 MHz	−122 to −2, +2 to +122	±11, ±39, ±75, ±103	242 total, 234 usable (3% pilots)	x4.9	x4.5
802.11ac, 160 MHz[a]	−250 to −130, −126 to −6, +6 to +126, +130 to +250	±25, ±53, ±89, ±117, ±139, ±167, ±203, ±231	484 total, 468 usable (3% pilots)	x9.75	x9.0

[a] For 80+80 MHz channels, the numbers are identical to the 160 MHz channel numbers.

Radio channel spectral mask

802.11ac channels have exactly the same shape as previous OFDM channels, differing only in the width of the energy transmitted. Figure 2-2 shows the general shape of an 802.11ac channel, which is described as decibels relative (dBr) to the peak level at the channel center frequency. The figure does not label the precise frequencies used because the spectral mask is the same shape no matter what size channel is used. Table 2-2 describes the key points on the spectral mask: the edge of the high-power peak, the start of the shoulder a few megahertz later, the point at which the shoulder steepens, and, finally, the point at which the background is reached.

Table 2-2. Spectral mask shape

Channel size	Edge of peak (0 dBr)	Start of shoulder (−20 dBr)	End of shoulder (−28 dBr)	Start of background (−40 dBr)
20 MHz	9 MHz	11 MHz	20 MHz	30 MHz
40 MHz	19	21	40	60
80 MHz	39	41	80	120
160 MHz	79	81	160	240

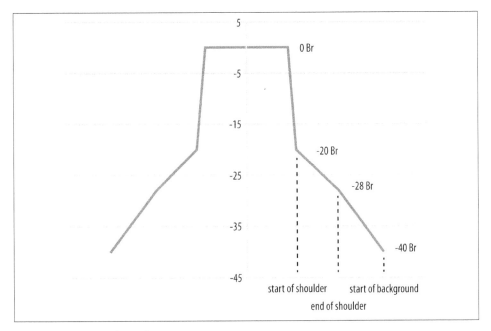

Figure 2-2. Spectral mask

Available Channel Map

Defining the available channels is more of a regulatory question than a technical one. Wireless LAN equipment is built with flexible radio chips that can tune to almost any frequency, and the 802.11 standards have defined a large number of channels. 802.11ac continues to use the same channel numbering defined by its predecessors, as illustrated in Figure 2-3. The top of the diagram identifies the frequency band and the channel numbers within that band. Channel numbers are spaced four digits apart, but within a wide channel, one of the frequencies is designated as the *primary channel*; others are called *secondary channels*. When used as part of an 80 MHz channel, channel 44 may be the primary channel, and channels 36, 40, and 48 will all be secondary channels. Generally speaking, when operating, a wireless LAN will send Beacon frames and announce its existence on its primary channel, but not on its secondary channels. Primary and secondary channels are important to bandwidth coexistence features, and will be discussed further in "Clear-Channel Assessment (CCA)" on page 45.

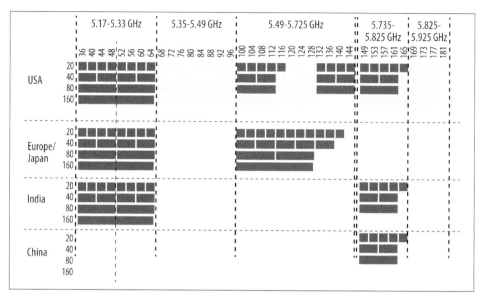

Figure 2-3. Available channel map for 802.11ac

As data has moved from existing wired LANs to wireless networks, additional spectrum has been made available. Regulators are generally aware of the need for additional spectrum, especially to make wider channels available for maximum speeds. The 802.11ac specification defines the channel numbering and layout, but the final say on whether a particular chunk of spectrum can be used lies with the national regulator.

Within Figure 2-3, there is a significant fraction of the spectrum depicted that represents proposed capacity for wireless LANs in the United States. In early 2013, the FCC acted to make a large amount of additional spectrum available. First, it acted to reclaim the "missing" channels between 120 and 128.[2] Second, the FCC moved to allocate two new bands for wireless LAN usage, shown here in the lighter shade, consisting of an additional 195 MHz of spectrum. As you can see from the figure, the FCC action stands to increase the amount of capacity available for 802.11ac by a significant amount. In fact, the proposed commission rules and statements by the commissioners themselves cited 802.11ac as a major driver for allocating this additional spectrum.

2. Within the 5.47–5.725 GHz band, wireless LANs are considered "secondary" users, meaning they must avoid interfering with the primary band users. One of the primary band users is Terminal-area Doppler Weather Radar (TDWR) at 5.600–5.650 GHz, a technology that monitors airport approaches for hazardous wind shear conditions. In 1985, Delta Air Lines flight 191 crashed after flying through storms. The crash directly led to onboard wind shear detection and the development of TDWR to assist pilots and air traffic controllers in avoiding these conditions. For more information, see my blog post on why we lost the weather radar channels (*http://blogs.aerohive.com/blog/the-wi-fi-security-blog/why-we-lost-the-weather-radar-channels*).

Proposed Additional Spectrum for 802.11ac in the United States

While this book was being written, the FCC proposed new rules that would dramatically increase the amount of spectrum available in the 5 GHz band. The first draft of the proposed rules was released on February 20, 2013.[3] The proposed rules go a long way to unifying the FCC rules in the 5 GHz band. Product developers will benefit from simpler rules, especially if the FCC action eventually leads to more consistent rules throughout the world. In the proposed rulemaking, the FCC specifically sought comment on how to work toward having one set of worldwide rules.

Even though 802.11 started off its life in the 2.4 GHz band that was originally considered to be "junk," the proposed rules illustrate how far 802.11 has come since it first came to market. Julius Genachowski, the FCC chairman at the time the new rules were proposed, has written and spoken extensively about how unlicensed spectrum fosters innovation, and the proposed rules reflect a broad consensus among the commission that enabling the further development of Wi-Fi is a useful goal.

Transmission: Modulation, Coding, and Guard Interval

Compared to prior 802.11 specifications, 802.11ac makes only evolutionary improvements to modulation and coding. Compared to its immediate predecessor, 802.11ac simplifies the selection of modulation and coding by discarding the rarely implemented unequal modulation options. Improved modulation technology provides one of the major points where 802.11ac picks up speed. Using the more aggressive 256-QAM modulation lets the link pack in two more bits on each carrier, for a total of eight bits instead of six. Adding two bits increases capacity by a third.

Modulation and Coding Set (MCS)

Selecting a modulation and coding set (MCS) is much simpler in 802.11ac than it was in 802.11n. Rather than the 70-plus options offered by 802.11n, the 802.11ac specification has only 10, shown in Table 2-3. The first seven are mandatory, and most vendors will support 256-QAM, and therefore all nine MCS options, in all products they bring to market. *Modulation* describes how many bits are contained within one transmission time increment. Higher modulations pack more data into the transmission, but they require much higher signal-to-noise ratios. Like its predecessors, 802.11ac uses an error-correcting code. One of the fundamental attributes of an error-correcting code is that it adds redundant information in a proportion described by the code rate. A code at rate

---

3. The Commission action to propose rules for this new spectrum, numbered FCC 13-22, is available at the FCC website (*http://hraunfoss.fcc.gov/edocs_public/attachmatch/FCC-13-22A1.docx*).

R=1/2 transmits one user data bit (the numerator) for every two bits (the denominator) on the channel. Higher code rates have more data and less redundancy at the cost of not being able to recover from as many errors. In 802.11ac, modulation and coding are coupled together into a single number, the MCS index. Each of the MCS values can lead to a wide range of speeds depending on the channel width, the number of spatial streams, and the guard interval. 802.11ac also does away with unequal modulation, a protocol feature from 802.11n that was not widely implemented.

Table 2-3. MCS values for 802.11ac

MCS index value	Modulation	Code rate (R)
0	BPSK	1/2
1	QPSK	1/2
2	QPSK	3/4
3	16-QAM	1/2
4	16-QAM	3/4
5	64-QAM	2/3
6	64-QAM	3/4
7	64-QAM	5/6
8	256-QAM	3/4
9	256-QAM	5/6

One of the ways that 802.11ac simplifies the selection of modulation and coding is that the modulation and coding are no longer tied to the number of spatial streams, as they were in 802.11n. To determine the link speed, knowledge of the MCS must be combined with both the number of streams to produce an overall data rate.

256-QAM modulation

Table 2-3 describes a new modulation for use with 802.11ac. Previous 802.11 standards allowed for up to 64-QAM, which allowed each transmission symbol to take on one of 64 values. At a high level, *quadrature amplitude modulation* (QAM) works by using the combination of amplitude level and phase shift to select one of many symbols in the *constellation.* To identify each of the 64 values, there are eight levels of inphase (roughly speaking, a phase shift) and eight levels of quadrature (roughly speaking, the amplitude of a wave). Each time a symbol is transmitted, it may take on one of eight phase shifts and one of eight amplitude levels.[4]

As with many other aspects of the protocol, 802.11ac kicks up the existing technology a notch by using 256-QAM. Rather than a constellation that is 8 by 8, the 256-QAM

---

4. There is a bit more to QAM than saying that it uses phase shifts and amplitude levels, but if you want to know the details, you are probably in a hardware engineering class or are a chip designer.

constellation has 16 phase shifts and 16 amplitude levels. Figure 2-4 compares the 64-QAM constellation to the 256-QAM constellation. At first glance, they're quite similar, though there are many more constellation points in the latter. One analogy that is often helpful is to compare QAM to a game of darts. The transmitter picks a target point and encodes an amplitude and phase shift. This amplitude and phase shift starts off at the ideal constellation point, and the receiver pulls the transmission out of the air and maps it onto what was received. As the constellation points get closer and closer together, the transmitter must be able to throw its darts much more accurately to hit the target point.

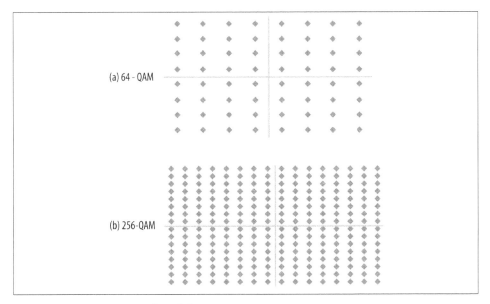

Figure 2-4. Comparison of modulations

The large number of extra points in the 256-QAM constellation point has the potential to dramatically improve speed. Instead of transmitting a maximum of six bits on each subcarrier in the channel, a 256-QAM-encoded link transmits eight bits. This single feature alone represents a 33% increase in speed over its nearest equivalent in 802.11n.

But nothing comes for free, and the 256-QAM speed boost is no exception. In order to use 256-QAM, the errors in the radio link must be much smaller than before. In a perfect link with ideal transmissions that are received absolutely error-free, the received points line up exactly on the constellation points, and it is easy to understand what should have been transmitted. Real-world radio links are never perfect, though. When a symbol is received, it does not line up exactly on the constellation point. The difference between the ideal constellation point and the point that corresponds to the received symbol exists in two-dimensional space, and therefore the "miss" is described by an *error vector*, as in Figure 2-5(a). When speaking about a transmission link, generally what system designers are concerned about is the size of the error and not its direction, so it is common to speak of the length of the error, which is called the *error vector magnitude* (EVM).

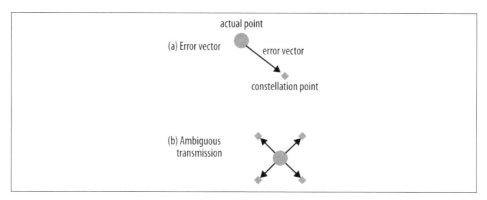

Figure 2-5. Error vectors

Not surprisingly, transmitting at 256-QAM requires much smaller errors than the less densely packed prior constellations. For example, when the received symbol is in the middle of several constellation points, such as in Figure 2-5(b), the receiver must choose one of the points. If it guesses wrong, the entire frame may need to be discarded. Early implementations of 802.11ac have shown that the required receiver performance for 256-QAM is a gain of about 5 dB over the 64-QAM receiver performance. To achieve better performance, there are a variety of techniques that can be applied. Higher-performance error-correcting codes can provide some of the required performance; 802.11ac includes a low-density parity check (LDPC) code that can provide a gain of 1–2 dB. Selecting better components for the analog frontend on the radio can also help. In addition to any distortions from the ideal point introduced by the radio channel itself, the receiver's analog section (antenna and amplifier) can also introduce distortion. Minimizing the introduction of errors in the analog section of an 802.11ac interface helps the digital section do its job better. Using LDPC and improving the analog frontend are not mutually exclusive, and some vendors will do both.

Guard Interval

802.11ac retains the ability to select a shortened OFDM guard interval if both the transmitter and the receiver are capable of processing it. With 802.11ac, it has exactly the same effect as in 802.11n: the guard interval shrinks from 800 ns to 400 ns, providing about a 10% boost in throughput. Most 802.11n deployments have proven capable of implementing the short guard interval without difficulty or adverse effects. Although the short guard interval is optional, I expect it to be widely supported, just as it was with 802.11n.[5]

Error-Correcting Codes

802.11ac does not make any changes to the supported error-correcting codes. Convolutional codes are required by 802.11ac, as they have been required for all OFDM PHYs. LDPC coding is supported as an option, and typically offers a gain of 1–2 dB over convolutional coding. Therefore, it is likely to be supported in combination with the very high data rates supported by 256-QAM and long packets transmitted in aggregate frames. By enabling higher data rates, LDPC will also assist in increasing the data rates. An increase in the data rate may enable a reduction in the transmission time, and hence an overall power savings.[6]

PHY-Level Framing

When designing the physical layer framing for 802.11ac, the protocol designers began by laying out requirements that the new frame needed to meet. Most importantly, it needed to be compatible with previous 802.11 PHYs. When an 802.11ac device transmits, 802.11a and 802.11n devices must be able to see and avoid the transmission for the length of time required on the medium. To meet this requirement, the format of the VHT physical layer frame is similar to the mixed-mode format used in 802.11n, and it begins with the same fields as 802.11a frames. A second subtle difference is required to enable multi-user MIMO transmissions, which is that the preamble must be able to describe the number of spatial streams and enable multiple receivers to set up to receive their frames. To meet this second requirement, a new physical layer header was required because the 802.11n HT-SIG header field was not readily extensible to new channel widths or large numbers of spatial streams.

Compared to 802.11n, the physical layer for 802.11ac is much simpler because there is only one format. Figure 2-6 shows the original non-HT format of an OFDM frame in Figure 2-6(a), along with the 802.11n mixed-mode frame format in Figure 2-6(b) and the VHT format in Figure 2-6(c).[7]

---

5. For more information on the short guard interval, see Chapter 3 of *802.11n: A Survival Guide*.

6. For more information on error-correcting codes, see Chapter 3 of *802.11n: A Survival Guide*.

7. For more information about the HT frame formats in 802.11n, see Chapter 3 of *802.11n: A Survival Guide*.

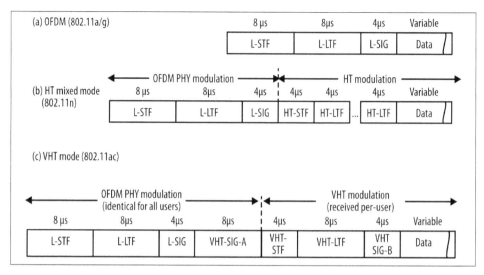

Figure 2-6. VHT physical layer frame format

The fields in the VHT frame are as follows:

Non-HT Short Training Field (L-STF) and Non-HT Long Training Field (L-LTF)
These fields are identical to the fields used in 802.11a; they consist of a sequence of 12 OFDM symbols that are used to assist the receiver in identifying that an 802.11 frame is about to start, synchronizing timers, and selecting an antenna. Any 802.11 device that is capable of OFDM operation can decode these fields.

Non-HT Signal Field (L-SIG)
The Signal field is used by 802.11a to describe the data rate and length (in bytes) of the frame, which is used by receivers to calculate the time duration of the frame's transmission. 802.11ac devices set the data rate to 6 Mbps and derive a spoofed length in bytes so that when any receiver calculates its length, it matches the time duration required for the 802.11ac frame.

VHT Signal A (VHT-SIG-A) and Signal B (VHT-SIG-B) Fields
The VHT Signal fields are the analog of the Signal field used in 802.11a or the HT Signal field used in 802.11n; however, they are understood only by 802.11ac devices. VHT signaling is split into two fields, the Signal A field and its companion, the Signal B field. Taken together, the two fields describe the included frame attributes such as the channel width, modulation and coding, and whether the frame is a single- or multi-user frame. Due to their complexity, these fields are described further in "The VHT Signal Fields" on page 23.

VHT Short Training Field (VHT-STF)

The VHT STF serves the same purpose as the non-HT STF. Just as the first training fields help a receiver tune in the signal, the VHT-STF assists the receiver in detecting a repeating pattern and setting receiver gain.

VHT Long Training Field (VHT-LTF)

The VHT long training field consists of a sequence of symbols that set up demodulation of the rest of the frame, starting with the VHT Signal B field. Depending on the number of transmitted streams, it consists of 1, 2, 4, 6, or 8 symbols; the number of required symbols is rounded up to the next highest even numbered value, so a link with five streams would use six symbols. This field's contents are also used for the channel estimation process that beamforming depends on.

Data field

The Data field holds the higher-layer protocol packet, or possibly an aggregate frame containing multiple higher-layer packets. This field is described in "The Data Field" on page 28. If no Data field is present in the physical layer payload, it is called a *null data packet* (NDP), which is used by the VHT PHY for beamforming setup, measurement, and tuning.

Null data packets are physical layer packets, not MAC layer packets. When a physical layer packet has no embedded payload, there is nothing for a MAC analyzer to report.

The VHT Signal Fields

All of the multi-carrier 802.11 PHYs use a Signal field to describe the payload of the physical layer frame, and 802.11ac is no exception. The purpose of the Signal field is to help the receiver decode the data payload, which is done by describing the parameters used for transmission. 802.11ac separates the signal into two different parts, called the Signal A and Signal B fields. The former is in the part of the physical layer header that is received identically by all receivers; the latter is in the part of the physical layer header that is different for each multi-user receiver.

VHT Signal A field

The Signal A field comes first in the frame, and it may take on one of two forms depending on whether the transmission is single-user or multi-user. The depiction of the Signal A field in Figure 2-7 is the format for a single user. (The multi-user format will be discussed in Chapter 4.) Because it holds rate information for decoding the payload of the physical layer frame, it is transmitted with the conservative BPSK modulation with a robust R=1/2 convolutional code. To be intelligible to other stations, it uses the modulation from the 802.11a OFDM PHY, which can transmit 24 bits of data per symbol. The two parts of the VHT Signal A field, each of which corresponds to an OFDM symbol, are referred to as VHT-SIG-A1 and VHT-SIG-A2. The two halves of the field are shown as Figure 2-7(a) and Figure 2-7(b), respectively. To assist a receiver in recognizing that the header belongs to a VHT frame, the constellation rotates between the two symbols.

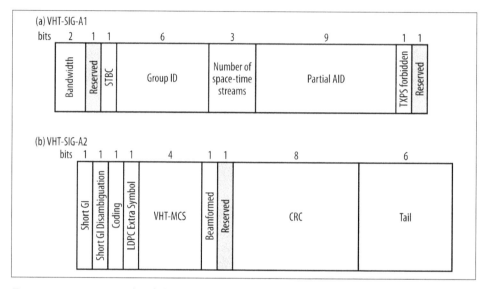

Figure 2-7. VHT Signal A field (single-user format)

The components of the Signal A field are:

Bandwidth (2 bits)
Two bits are used to indicate the channel bandwidth: 0 for 20 MHz, 1 for 40 MHz, 2 for 80 MHz, and 3 for 160 MHz.

STBC (1 bit)
If the payload is encoded with space-time block coding (STBC)[8] for extra robustness, this field will be 1. Otherwise, it will be 0.

Group ID (6 bits)
When transmitting a single-user frame, this field will be 0 or 63. This field enables a receiver to determine whether the data payload is single- or multi-user. A group ID of 0 is used for frames sent to an AP, and a group ID of 63 is used for frames sent to a client.

---

8. STBC may be used when the number of radio chains exceeds the number of spatial streams; it transmits a single data stream across two spatial streams. In effect, it takes MIMO gain and translates it into increased range.

Number of space-time streams (3 bits)

This field indicates the number of space-time streams, but the field is zero-based. Therefore, the number of space-time streams will be one greater than the binary value of this field. For example, if the field is the number 3, then there are four space-time streams.

Partial AID (9 bits)

For transmissions to an AP, the partial AID is the last nine bits of the BSSID. For a client, the partial AID is an identifier that combines the association ID and the BSSID of its serving AP.

Transmit power save forbidden (1 bit)

If the access point in a network allows client devices to power off radios when they have the opportunity to transmit frames, this field will be 0. Otherwise, it is 1.

Short GI (1 bit)

This field is set to 1 to indicate that the 400 ns short guard interval is used for the data payload of the physical layer frame. Otherwise, it is 0.

Short GI disambiguation (1 bit)

When the short guard interval is used, an extra symbol might be needed for the payload of the physical layer frame. A single bit is used to indicate whether the extra symbol is required (1) or not (0).

Coding (1 bit)

This field is 0 when convolutional coding is used to protect the Data field, and 1 when LDPC is used.

LDPC extra symbol (1 bit)

LDPC coding can create the need for an extra OFDM symbol to transmit the Data field. If this field is set to 1, it indicates the extra symbol is required.

MCS (4 bits)

This field contains the MCS index value for the payload, as shown in the first column of Table 2-3.

Beamformed (1 bit)

When a beamforming matrix is applied to the transmission, this bit is set to 1; otherwise, it is set to 0.

CRC (8 bits)

The CRC allows the receiver of the physical layer frame to detect errors in the Signal A field.

Tail (6 bits)

Six zeros are included to terminate the convolutional coder that protects the Signal A field. Convolutional codes require a "ramp down" of trailing zeros to function properly.

VHT Signal B field

The VHT Signal B field is used to set up the data rate, as well as tune in MIMO reception. Like the VHT Signal A field, it is modulated conservatively to assist receivers in determining the data rate of the payload; however, it is modulated using the VHT MCS 0. Although it is modulated with BPSK with a convolutional code of R=1/2, the VHT modulations have slightly more efficiency and hold a few more bits. The VHT Signal B field is designed to be transmitted in a single OFDM symbol, which is why it has slightly different lengths depending on the channel width. Figure 2-8 shows the single-user format of the VHT Signal B field and its dependence on channel width. (Other formats for this field will be discussed in Chapter 4.)

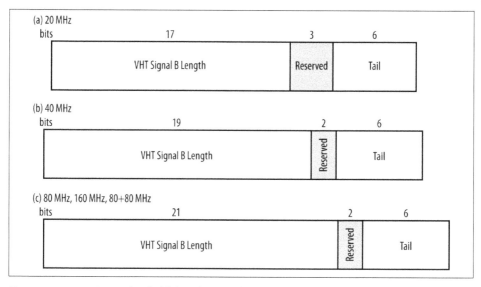

Figure 2-8. VHT Signal B field (single-user format)

In its single-user form, the raw VHT Signal B field is either 26, 27, or 29 bits, depending on the channel width, and consists of the following fields:

VHT Signal B Length (17, 19, or 21 bits)

This field measures the length of the Data field payload of the physical layer frame, in four-byte units. This field varies in size so that the maximum value of the field is an approximately constant duration in time (a 40 MHz channel is capable of transmitting much more data in the payload field, and thus needs a longer-length field). The reason why this field measures not the actual number of bytes but the number of four-byte chunks is for efficiency, as will be explained in "Frame Size and Aggregation" on page 38.

Reserved bits (2 or 3 bits)
The bits between the length field and the tail are reserved, and must be set to 1.

Tail bits (6 bits)
Six zero bits are included to allow the convolutional coder to complete.

There is no CRC within the VHT Signal B field. To detect errors in the VHT Signal B field, there is a CRC at the start of the Data field, which will be described in the next section.

To transmit the VHT Signal B field, it is expanded to fill the available space within one symbol. Wider channels have the capacity to carry more data, so the Signal B field is repeated, as shown in Figure 2-9. For a 40 MHz channel, the field is repeated once. For an 80 MHz channel, the field is repeated three times and a pad bit of 0 is appended. For a 160 MHz (or an 80+80 MHz) channel, the field is repeated four times, a pad bit of 0 is added, and then the resulting structure is repeated once. This process of repeating the signal field ensures that it occupies exactly one symbol.

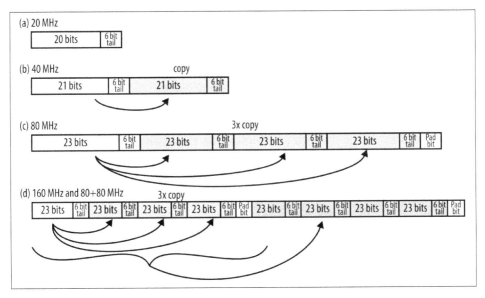

Figure 2-9. VHT Signal B expansion

The Data Field

Immediately following the physical layer header, the Data field begins to transmit the payload of the physical layer frame. The format of the Data field is shown in Figure 2-10. Because the Data field is transmitted following the header, it is transmitted at the data rate described by the physical layer header. The Data field carries a frame from higher protocol layers.

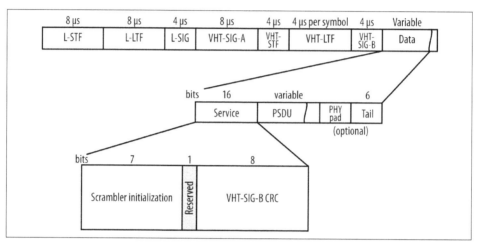

Figure 2-10. Physical layer data encoding

Before beginning transmission of the data from higher-layer protocols, there are a few housekeeping fields embedded in the physical layer frame:

Service (16 bits)
> The Service field is prepended to the higher-level protocol data before transmission. It consists of seven bits to initialize a data scrambler to avoid long runs of identical bits and a CRC of the VHT Signal B field to detect errors.

PHY Service Data Unit (PSDU), or frame from MAC layer
> The PSDU field contains a frame from from the 802.11 MAC layer. It is variable length.

PHY pad
> To ensure that the number of bits passed to the transmitter will exactly match the number of bits required for a symbol, pad bits are added.

Tail
> Tail bits are present when the physical layer frame is protected with a convolutional code and are used to ramp down the convolutional coder. If LDPC is used, the tail bits are not required.

The Transmission and Reception Process

A block diagram for an 802.11ac interface is shown in Figure 2-11. This block diagram can be used to transmit both single-user and multi-user frames, but this chapter focuses on the single-user transmission use case.

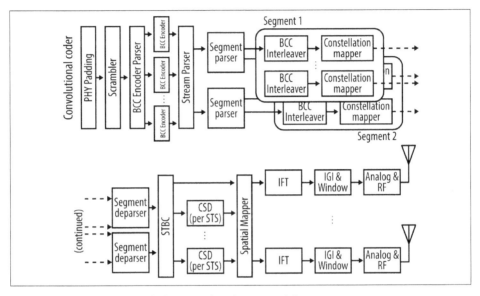

Figure 2-11. 802.11ac block diagram (single-user only)

When the MAC presents a frame for transmission, it is passed to the physical layer, and the following procedure is run:

1. **Preparation of Service field**. To begin, the Service field that is prepended to the data for transmission is constructed. The main component of the Service field is the CRC calculated over the contents of the VHT-SIG-B field.

2. **PHY padding**. The first step in transmission is to pad the frame so that its length matches the number of bits required to end on a physical-level symbol boundary.

3. **Scrambling and forward error correction (FEC) encoding**. The scrambler reduces the probability of long strings of identical bits in its output, and is present because convolutional codes work best on data that does not have long runs of identical bits. The output of the scrambler is fed to a FEC encoder, which may be either a convolutional coder or an LDPC encoder. To achieve many different code rates, a single-rate FEC encoder's output may be *punctured* to achieve higher-rate codes.[9]

---

9. For more information on puncturing, see Chapter 13 of *802.11 Wireless Networks: The Definitive Guide.*

4. **Stream parsing**. The stream parser takes the output of the FEC encoder and divides up the encoded bits between each spatial stream. For example, if there are two spatial streams, the stream parser will divide up the encoded bits and assign each of them to one of the spatial streams. At this point, the bits flowing from the stream parser to the interleaver are a *spatial stream*. Output from the stream parser is sent to the interleaver, which is the first component in the radio chain.

5. **Segment parsing**. All 160 MHz transmissions, whether using a contiguous 160 MHz block or two 80 MHz blocks, are mapped into two 80 MHz *frequency segments*. Segment parsing is not performed on 20 MHz, 40 MHz, or 80 MHz transmissions.

6. **Convolutional code interleaving**. Convolutional codes work best when errors are isolated, and errors on radio channels tend to affect several bits in a row. The interleaver takes sequential bits from the carriers and separates them in the convolutional code bitstream to separate errors and make them easier to correct. (LDPC has a similar function executed after constellation mapping.)

7. **Constellation mapping**. Bits are mapped onto QAM constellation points using the selected modulation. When denser modulations such as 64-QAM or 256-QAM are used, more bits are mapped at a time.

8. **LDPC tone mapping**. Tone mapping takes constellation points and ensures they are mapped to OFDM subcarriers separated by a sufficient distance. It serves the same purpose as the interleaver for convolutional codes. For example, in a 40 MHz channel, two consecutive constellation points must be separated by at least six OFDM subcarriers to ensure that interference must be about 1.5 MHz wide to interfere with successive bits.

9. **Segment deparsing**. For 160 MHz channels, the segment deparser brings the two frequency segments back together for transformation from constellation symbols into a set of spatial streams suitable for transmission.

10. **Space-time block coding (STBC)**. This optional step is used to transmit one spatial stream across multiple antennas for extra redundancy. The space-time block coder takes a single constellation symbol output and maps it onto multiple radio chains, transforming the spatial streams into *space-time streams*.[10]

11. **Pilot insertion and cyclic shift diversity (CSD)**. Constellation points for transmission are combined with the data for pilot subcarriers to create the complete data set for transmission. When multiple data streams are present, they are each given a small phase shift to aid in distinguishing between them at the receiver. The phase shift is referred to as *cyclic shift diversity* because a slightly different phase shift is applied to each of the space-time streams.

---

10. For more information on STBC, see Chapter 4 of *802.11n: A Survival Guide*.

---

12. **Spatial mapping**. Space-time streams are mapped onto the transmit chains by the spatial mapper. The simplest approach is a *direct mapping* that turns a spatial stream into a space-time stream for a single transmit chain. For higher performance, the spatial mapper may spread all of the space-time streams on to all of the transmission chains in a *spatial expansion*. This process is a key component of beamforming, which can be used to shape a space-time stream to direct energy in the direction of a receiver.[11]

13. **Inverse Fourier transform (IFT)**. An inverse Fourier transform takes frequency-domain data from OFDM and converts it to time-domain data for transmission.

14. **Guard insertion and windowing**. The guard interval is inserted at the start of each symbol, and each symbol is windowed to improve signal quality at the receiver.

15. **Preamble construction**. The VHT preamble consisting of the non-VHT-modulated training fields (see Figure 2-6(c)) is constructed. The preamble is created for each 20 MHz channel within the transmission channel. To guard against interference, each of the 20 MHz segments of the preamble are given a slight cyclic delay.

16. **RF and analog section**. This prepares the data for transmission out an antenna, following the VHT preamble. The complex waveform that comes from the previous step is converted to a signal that can be placed on a carrier at the center frequency of the channel selected by the current AP. A high power amplifier (HPA) increases the power so the signal can travel as far as needed, within regulatory limits.

Receiving frames is the inverse of the transmission process. Incoming signals from the antenna are amplified by a low-noise amplifier (LNA) on each radio chain, and the preamble is used to set up the receiver to adjust for any frequency-specific fades that occur in the channel. After compensating for the channel based on the reception of the preamble and pilot carriers, the incoming data is a series of constellation symbols. If STBC was used for transmission, multiple streams of constellation symbols will be combined into a single output bitstream; otherwise, each space-time stream becomes its own stream of constellation symbols. Constellation symbols are turned into bits and processed by the FEC decoder, which will (hopefully) correct any resulting errors. The resulting bitstream can be descrambled into a MAC frame and passed to the MAC for further processing.

11. A spatial expansion takes a given number of space-time streams and maps them onto transmit chains by using a matrix multiplication. Because the matrix multiplication can affect how much energy is directed from each transmission chain, the matrix is sometimes called a *steering matrix* when it is used to direct beam energy.

Single Spatial Stream Operation

Single-stream transmission is substantially simpler than multi-stream operation. When a device transmits multiple spatial streams, significant computational resources are applied to combine multiple spatial streams into one transmission. With only one spatial stream, however, the digital signal processing (DSP) work is not needed. Eliminating the DSP requirement also substantially reduces power consumption, which is why many small battery-operated devices are single-stream only.

802.11ac Data Rates

Answering the question "How fast does 802.11ac go?" is not straightforward. Data rates are determined by the combination of channel width, modulation and coding, number of spatial streams, and the guard interval. About 5% of 802.11ac draft 2.0 was devoted to tables that answer this question. It's not useful to create exhaustive tables or complex formulas. Instead, I'll take it in terms of a few numbers that tend to stick out:

400 Mbps (two spatial streams at 40 MHz short guard interval)
This is a full third faster than the comparable 802.11n data rate.

900 Mbps (two spatial streams at 80 MHz, short guard interval)
Technically, it's only 867 Mbps, but it's nicer to round up and get that much closer to 1 Gbps. I expect the first generation of products will be able to achieve this data rate, though the range at which they will do so is still to be determined.

1 Gbps
This isn't a data rate in the specification itself, but it represents a readily achievable target in high-end equipment. With the same three spatial streams as you get in mainstream 802.11n equipment, you can get to 1.3 Gbps. Or, with four-stream 802.11ac and 80 MHz channels, you can get to 1 Gbps while still using 64-QAM.

802.11ac Data Rate Matrix

Another way to look at the speeds of 802.11ac is to work from a "baseline" speed. At its most basic level, 802.11ac can transmit a single spatial stream in a 20 MHz channel, and the speed of that single spatial stream can be related to many higher data rates through simple mathematical operations. Each spatial stream adds proportionally to throughput. Wider channels also increase throughput proportionally. To get the speed of any MCS rate, take the basic 20 MHz stream, multiply by the number of spatial streams, and then multiply that result by a channel correction factor. Table 2-4 shows how the calculation works. Take the MCS value from the lefthand column, and translate that to the building block data rate in the second column. Multiply by the indicated factors in the next two columns to work out the resulting data rate. The three rightmost columns show the maximum data rates standardized in 802.11ac.

Table 2-4. 802.11ac data rate matrix

MCS value	20 MHz data rate (1SS, short GI)	Spatial stream multiplication factor	Channel width multiplication factor	Maximum 40 MHz rate (8 SS, short GI)	Maximum 80 MHz rate (8 SS, short GI)	Maximum 160 MHz rate (8 SS, short GI)
MCS 0	7.2 Mbps	x2 for 2 streams	x1.0 for 20 MHz	120.0 Mbps	260.0 Mbps	520.0 Mbps
MCS 1	14.4	x3 for 3 streams	x2.1 for 40 MHz	240.0	520.0	1040.0
MCS 2	21.7	x4 for 4 streams	x4.5 for 80 MHz	360.0	780.0	1560.0
MCS 3	28.9	x5 for 5 streams	x9.0 for 160 MHz	480.0	1040.0	2080.0
MCS 4	43.3	x6 for 6 streams		720.0	1560.0	3120.0
MCS 5	57.8	x7 for 7 streams		960.0	2080.0	4160.0
MCS 6	65.0	x8 for 8 streams		1080.0	2340.0	4680.0
MCS 7	72.2			1200.0	2600.0	5200.0
MCS 8	86.7			1440.0	3120.0	6240.0
MCS 9	96.3[a]			1600.0	3466.7	6933.3

[a] MCS 9 is not allowed for a single stream using a 20 MHz channel, as will be described in the next section.

"Missing" MCS values

The 802.11ac standard has several MCS values that are listed as "Not valid" without further explanation, which are listed in Table 2-5. Roughly speaking, these combinations of MCS and channel width do not cleanly fit within the boundaries of the encoding and interleaving process used to assemble a frame.

Table 2-5. Invalid 802.11ac MCS values

	20 MHz	80 MHz	160 MHz
MCS 6	n/a	3 and 7 SS	n/a
MCS 9	1, 2, 4, 5, 7, and 8 SS	6 SS	3 SS

To understand why these combinations do not cleanly fit on an encoding boundary, consider the flow of data from higher layers down to symbols, as illustrated in Figure 2-12. Input data first is processed by a forward error correction code. Error-correction codes work by adding redundant bits to recover errors; an R=5/6 code will encode five "data" bits from higher-layer protocols and transmit six "coded" bits. In 802.11ac, multiple encoders each produce an encoding stream, and the output of each encoder is mapped onto each of the subcarrier channels.

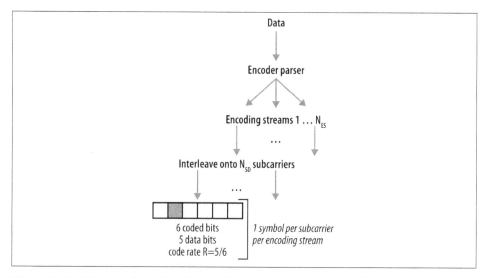

Figure 2-12. 802.11ac data flow from higher-level protocols to symbols

The modulation defines the number of coded bits available per subcarrier. With 256-QAM operating on a 20 MHz channel, for example, there are 416 coded bits available per subcarrier. When the code rate is 3/4, as in MCS 8, the 416 coded bits are broken up into 104 blocks. When the code rate is 5/6, however, the 416 coded bits do not cleanly break into a series of blocks. There are 69 blocks of 6 bits, with 2 bits left over. The 802.11ac task group elected not to add padding, and simply listed the resulting data rate as not valid.

Roughly speaking, the rule for determining whether an MCS will be valid is that the number of coded bits per subcarrier must be an integer multiple of the number of encoding streams. Furthermore, the number of coded bits per encoding stream must be an integer multiple of the denominator in the code rate.[12]

Simplifying Modulation Options in 802.11ac

One of the reasons that 802.11ac has many fewer options for MCS values than 802.11n is that the MCS value is no longer tied to the number of spatial streams. In 802.11n, MCS 0 and MCS 8 both use BPSK with R=1/2. In 802.11ac, the MCS value is defined only as a modulation and code set, and no longer includes the number of spatial streams. The second way that 802.11ac simplified the MCS selection is that it dropped the unequal modulation option (802.11n MCS values from 33 to 76).

---

12. For the full details, see slide 4 of 802.11 document 11-10/0820r0 (*http://bit.ly/1abp0Zj*), which lays out the framework for MCS selection, and 802.11 document 11-11/0577r1 (*http://bit.ly/12E9T5a*), which proposed filling in some of the data rate holes in 802.11ac by increasing the number of encoders within products.

Unequal modulation is specified in 802.11n to support beamforming. Transmit beamforming in the form used by 802.11 results in each spatial stream having a different signal-to-noise ratio (SNR). Unequal modulation was designed so that high-SNR streams could use high-data-rate modulation options, and low-SNR streams could use low-data-rate modulation options. As an example, 802.11n MCS 42 modulates one stream at 64-QAM, one stream at 16-QAM, and one using QPSK; this modulation was intended for use with one high-SNR stream, one medium-SNR stream, and one low-SNR stream.

802.11ac eliminated unequal modulation as part of its simplification of data rates, and as a result, 802.11ac transmit beamforming requires that all spatial streams be modulated identically.

Comparison of 802.11ac Data Rates to Other 802.11 PHYs

For another view, see Table 2-6, which compares the highest possible data rate for several wireless technology combinations. The table compares the top data rate, not necessarily a typical data rate. 802.11ac speeds are quoted using 256-QAM, which may not always be achievable in real-world deployments.

Table 2-6. Speed comparisons between different 802.11 standards

Technology	20 MHz[a]	40 MHz	80 MHz	160 MHz
802.11b	11 Mbps			
802.11a/g	54 Mbps			
802.11n (1 SS)	72 Mbps	150 Mbps		
802.11ac (1 SS)	87 Mbps	200 Mbps	433 Mbps	867 Mbps
802.11n (2 SS)	144 Mbps	300 Mbps		
802.11ac (2 SS)	173 Mbps	400 Mbps	867 Mbps	1.7 Gbps
802.11n (3 SS)	216 Mbps	450 Mbps		
802.11ac (3 SS)	289 Mbps	600 Mbps	1.3 Gbps	2.3 Gbps[b]
802.11n (4 SS)[c]	289 Mbps	600 Mbps		
802.11ac (4 SS)	347 Mbps	800 Mbps	1.7 Gbps	3.5 Gbps
802.11ac (8 SS)	693 Mbps	1.6 Gbps	3.4 Gbps	6.9 Gbps

[a] MCS 9 is not valid for 802.11ac in 20 MHz channels, so the 20 MHz values for 802.11ac are MCS 8.

[b] MCS 9 is not valid for a three-stream 802.11ac device with 160 MHz channels, so this is the (lower) value for MCS 8.

[c] Four-stream 802.11n products were never released widely. I expect the market to leapfrog four-stream 11n for four-stream 11ac; this line in the table is included for comparison purposes.

Mandatory PHY Features

802.11ac is a complex specification with a large number of protocol features. Table 2-7 classifies the protocol features as either mandatory or optional. As a general principle, the Wi-Fi Alliance certification programs validate mandatory functionality in the specification, and create optional tests only for the most widely supported and high-value features.

Table 2-7. Feature classification of PHY features

Feature	Mandatory/ Optional	Comments
Support for VHT format of frames	Mandatory	
20 & 40 MHz channels	Mandatory	These channel widths were required in previous PHY standards.
80 MHz channels	Mandatory	
160 MHz and 80+80 MHz operation	Optional	Not supported by first wave of devices.
Single-stream operation MCS 0 through 7	Mandatory	
Single-stream operation MCS 8 and 9	Optional	Optional, but likely to be widely supported.
Two-stream operation	Optional	Mandatory in WFA program for anything other than a battery-operated mobile AP, just as with 802.11n certification.
Three-stream operation	Optional	
Four-stream operation	Optional	
Five- to eight-stream operation	Optional	Not likely to be supported until later product releases.
Support for MCS 8 and 9 (256-QAM) with more than one stream	Optional	
Short guard interval of 400 ns	Optional	Although optional, this will be widely supported. (Approximately 3/4 of WFA-certified 11n devices implement the feature.)
LDPC	Optional	Likely to be supported in tandem with 256-QAM.
STBC	Optional	Likely to be moderately well supported, but most products will implement only single-stream (2x1) operation.

CHAPTER 3

The MAC

If you cannot get rid of the family skeleton,
you might as well make it dance.

—George Bernard Shaw

Most of the work in the 802.11ac MAC is evolutionary. In contrast with the major efficiency enhancements introduced in 802.11n, most of the MAC work in 802.11ac consists of supporting new physical layer features. Frames are bigger, but the aggregation framework in place handles those larger frames without significant change. One of the few protocol features to see large changes was around sharing radio resources between channels of different sizes.

Framing

For the most part, 802.11ac maintains the frame format used by its predecessors. There are two major changes, shown in Figure 3-1. First, 802.11ac extends the maximum frame size from almost 8,000 bytes to over 11,000 bytes, further increasing the ability to aggregate frames from higher layers. Second, it reuses the HT Control field from 11n, but does so by defining a new form of the Control field. When the HT Control field begins with a 0, the format is identical to 802.11n and the HT Control field is of the *HT-variant* type.[1] When the HT Control field begins with a 1, the HT Control field is of the *VHT-variant* type. Figure 3-1 shows the format of the VHT-variant HT Control field. It is composed of fields that are used to communicate *MCS feedback*, a seldom-implemented procedure that enables two devices to exchange information on how well transmissions are received to find the best data rate for the connection.

---

1. For the format of the HT-variant HT Control field, see Figure 5-1 in *802.11n: A Survival Guide*.

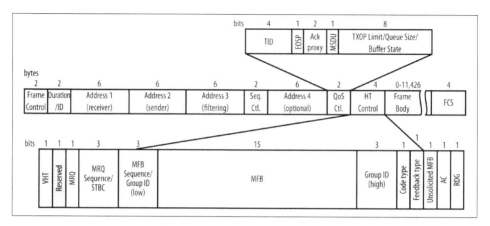

Figure 3-1. 802.11ac MAC frame format

Frame Size and Aggregation

Frame aggregation was introduced in 802.11n to improve network efficiency. As with many network protocols, one of the biggest sources of overhead in 802.11 is acquiring the channel for the right to transmit. Aggregation works to decrease the relative amount of overhead by allowing a device to obtain access to the radio channel and then using that opportunity to transmit multiple frames.[2] 802.11 standards are not prescriptive and define only the aggregate frame format. Implementing aggregation requires that a device look ahead through its transmit queue to find frames to coalesce into a single aggregate frame, and each vendor's implementation may be slightly different.

802.11ac, however, adds an interesting new take on aggregation: all frames transmitted use the aggregate MPDU (A-MPDU) format. Even a single frame transmitted in one shot is transmitted as an aggregate frame. Moving to an all-aggregate, all-the-time transmission model means that the 802.11ac MAC must take over all the framing responsibility, and the physical layer works only with the total length of what it transports.

All 802.11ac data frames are sent in an A-MPDU, even if the A-MPDU has only one frame in it.

---

2. 802.11ac does not add any new aggregation methods; for an introduction to the use of aggregation in 802.11, see Chapter 5 of *802.11n: A Survival Guide*.

It might seem at first glance that transmitting every frame as an A-MPDU, regardless of the content of the data, would not be efficient. However, due to the potentially high speeds in 802.11ac, simply describing the length of the frame requires a large number of bits. The maximum transmission length is defined by time, and is a little less than 5.5 milliseconds. At the highest data rates for 802.11ac, an aggregate frame can hold almost four and a half megabytes of data. Rather than represent such a large number of bytes in the PLCP header, which is transmitted at the lowest possible data rate, 802.11ac shifts the length indication to the MPDU delimiters that are transmitted as part of the high-data-rate payload.[3]

Figure 3-2 shows the format of the A-MPDU aggregation type. The maximum length of an A-MPDU is controlled by the value of a field called the *Maximum A-MPDU Length Exponent*, which describes the maximum length of an A-MPDU by the formula $2^{13+\text{Exponent}}-1$ bytes. 802.11ac allows values for the exponent ranging from 0 to 7, which allows the maximum A-MPDU length to range from 8 KB to 1 MB.[4] Table 3-1 compares the amount of data that can be transmitted at various points in the protocol stack by the 5 GHz–capable 802.11 physical layers.

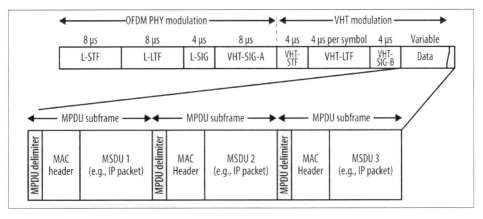

Figure 3-2. A-MPDU aggregation for efficiency

3. Describing 4.5 MB of data requires 23 bits of information in the header. Practically speaking, putting that information in the VHT Signal header would require expanding it to be two OFDM symbols, which would add 4 μs to each frame. By putting timing information in the VHT Signal header and moving the byte field into the high-rate modulated data field, the efficiency of the network is increased.

4. 802.11n allowed values from 0 to 3, which capped the maximum A-MPDU at 64 KB.

Table 3-1. Size comparisons of transmissions for different 802.11 PHYs

Attribute	802.11a	802.11n	802.11ac
MSDU (MAC payload) size	2,304	2,304	2,304
MPDU (MAC frame) size	Implied by maximum MSDU size	Implied by A-MSDU size	11,454
A-MSDU (aggregate MAC payload) size	Not used with 802.11a	7,935	Implied by maximum MPDU size
PSDU (PLCP payload) size	4,095 bytes	65,535 bytes	4,692,480 bytes
PPDU (PLCP frame) size	Implied by maximum PSDU size	5.484 ms (mixed mode) or 10 ms (greenfield mode)	5.484 ms

Management Frames

Management frames signal that they are capable of building an 802.11ac network or participating in an 802.11ac network by including the VHT Capabilities Information element. This element is placed in Probe Request and Probe Response frames to enable client devices to match their capabilities to those offered by a wireless network.

The VHT Capabilities Information element

The VHT Capabilities Information element, shown in Figure 3-3, is the core information element used in management frames to set up operation of 802.11ac networks. It has a simple structure, consisting of two fields that describe the protocol features supported by the transmitter and the speeds that the transmitter is capable of using.

Within the VHT Capabilities Info element, the fields are:

Maximum MPDU Length (2 bits)
> MAC frames in 802.11ac may have one of three lengths: 3,895 bytes, 7,991 bytes, or 11,454 bytes. Those three lengths correspond to values of 0, 1, and 2 in this field. The value of 3 is reserved.

Supported Channel Width set (2 bits)
> 802.11ac devices are required to support 20 MHz, 40 MHz, and 80 MHz operation. This field is used to indicate support for 160 MHz operation. It takes on the value 0 if there is no 160 MHz support, the value 1 if the transmitter supports 160 MHz contiguous operation only, and the value 2 if it supports both 160 MHz contiguous operation and 80+80 MHz operation. The value 3 is reserved.

Rx LDPC (1 bit)
> This field is set to 1 if the transmitter can receive LDPC-encoded frames.

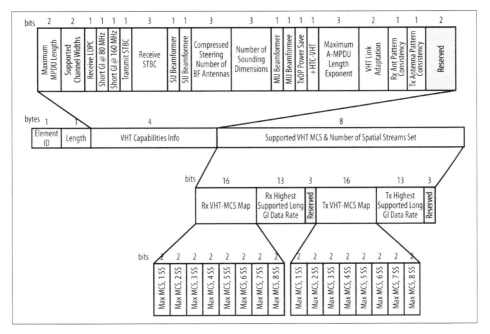

Figure 3-3. VHT Capabilities Information element

Short GI for 80 (1 bit) and Short GI for 160 & 80+80 (1 bit)

These fields are each set to 1 if the transmitter can receive frames transmitted using the short guard interval with the indicated channel bandwidth. See "Guard Interval" on page 20 for more details.

Tx STBC (1 bit)

This field is set to 1 to indicate that transmission of STBC-coded frames is supported.

Rx STBC (3 bits)

This field describes how many spatial streams are supported for reception of STBC-coded frames. It may be set to 0, 1, 2, 3, or 4, describing the maximum number of spatial streams supported on reception.[5] For support of one spatial stream, the field takes the value 1. The value 0 is used to indicate that STBC is not supported, and the values 5–7 are reserved.

---

5. STBC spreads a single spatial stream across two transmit chains and two space-time streams. Therefore, an eight-stream-capable device can transmit a maximum of four spatial streams when STBC is used.

Single-User (SU) Beamformer (1 bit) and Beamformee (1 bit)
When set to 1, these fields indicate that the transmitter is capable of operating as a single-user beamformer or beamformee that exchanges packets with one other station. This feature will be discussed in Chapter 4.

Compressed Steering Number of Beamformer (BF) Antennas (3 bits) and Number of Sounding Dimensions (3 bits)
These fields are used in the channel measurement process for beamforming to indicate the maximum number of antennas that can participate in channel measurement, and will be described more fully in Chapter 4.

Multi-User (MU) Beamformer (1 bit) and Beamformee (1 bit)
When set to 1, these fields indicate that the transmitter is capable of operating as a multi-user beamformer or beamformee.

VHT TxOp Power-Save (1 bit)
An AP can set this bit to 1 to enable power save operations during a VHT transmission burst, or 0 to disable them. Stations associating with a network will set this bit to 1 to indicate the capability is enabled or 0 if it is disabled.

+HTC-VHT capable (1 bit)
This value is set to 1 to indicate that the transmitter is capable of receiving the VHT-variant HT Control field.

Max A-MPDU Length Exponent (3 bits)
This field can take on the values 0–7 and is used to communicate the size of the A-MPDU that may be transmitted. The effects of its values are described in "Frame Size and Aggregation" on page 38.

VHT Link Adaptation capable (2 bits)
This field is used for link adaptation feedback to select the most appropriate MCS for a link using explicit feedback.

Receive and Transmit Antenna Pattern Consistency (1 bit each)
These bits are each set to 1 if the antenna pattern of the transmitter does not change after association completes, and 0 otherwise. One of the most common reasons for an antenna pattern to change is beamforming.

Following the Capabilities element is the Supported MCS Set element, shown at the bottom of Figure 3-3. It is split into two identical halves, with the first half describing the receiving capabilities and the second half describing the transmission capabilities. It contains the following fields:

Rx and Tx VHT-MCS Map (16 bits each)
The MCS map is a simple structure. Two bits are used to represent three options: the value 0 stands for the mandatory minimum support of MCS 0 through 7, the value of 1 adds MCS 8 for a total support of MCS 0 through 8, and the value of 2

adds MCS 9 for total support of MCS 0 through 9. The value of 3 is reserved. The two-bit field repeats eight times so that the transmitter can specify the maximum MCS supported for each spatial stream.

Rx and Tx Highest Supported Data Rate (13 bits each)
These 13-bit fields represent the highest total data rate supported, in units of 1 Mbps. For example, a device that supported a maximum speed of 867 Mbps (80 MHz channels with two spatial streams) would set this field to 0001101100011, which is 867 in binary notation. This field has the length of 13 bits because 13 bits allows representation of up to 8,191 Mbps, which is beyond the maximum data rate in 802.11ac.

 Because the MCS map field only allows three options (MCS 0 through 7, MCS 0 through 8, and MCS 0 through 9), it is not possible to disable low data rates in an 11ac network.

The VHT Operation Information element

All 802.11 physical layers have an information element (IE) that describes their operation, and the VHT PHY is no exception. The VHT Operation IE, shown in Figure 3-4, describes the channel information and the basic rates supported by the transmitter. Basic rates are those rates that are supported by all clients attached to an AP, and therefore are safe to use for frames that are destined for a group of multiple stations. Rate support, which is found in the second field of the IE, is transmitted identically to the rate support in the VHT Capabilities IE. The first part of the information element describes the channels used by the transmitter through the following fields:

Channel Width (1 byte)
For either 20 MHz or 40 MHz operation, the Channel Width field is set to 0. 80 MHz operation sets this value to 1. Because it is necessary to distinguish the 160 MHz channel width (a value of 2) from the 80+80 MHz channel structure (a value of 3), they receive separate values. All other values of this field are reserved.

Channel Center Frequency 0 (1 byte)
This fields are used only with 80 and 160 MHz operation, to transmit the center channel frequency of the BSS. In 80+80 MHz operation, it is the center channel frequency of the lower frequency segment.

Channel Center Frequency 1 (1 byte)
This field is used only with 80+80 MHz operation, and is used to transmit the center channel frequency of the second segment.

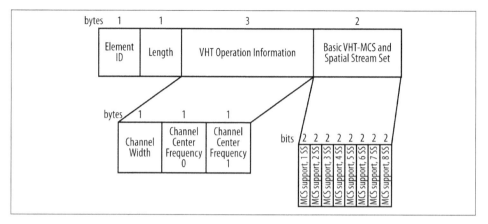

Figure 3-4. VHT Operation Information element

Other management frame changes

In addition to communicating capabilities and operating status, some other minor changes were made to management frames and management protocols in 802.11ac:

- The *Transmit Power Envelope* element enables APs to communicate transmission power limits for each of the available channel bandwidths.

- The *Channel Switch Wrapper* element extends the existing channel-switch announcements by enabling a channel switch announcement frame to not only direct devices to a new channel, but also state the channel bandwidth.

- The *Extended BSS Load* element enables an AP to describe the amount of time spent transmitting on each channel bandwidth so that a receiver can see how much time is spent on 20, 40, 80, and 160 MHz operations.

- The *Operating Mode Notification* element describes the current channel width and number of spatial streams active.

Medium Access Procedures

In keeping with its evolutionary nature, 802.11ac does not introduce significant new changes to the way that devices access the network medium. However, with new channel bandwidths come new rules for determining whether the channel is clear. To make the most efficient use of spectrum, 802.11ac also adds new rules for allowing devices to indicate their intended bandwidth consumption in RTS/CTS exchanges.

Clear-Channel Assessment (CCA)

802.11 has always been a "listen-before-talk" protocol in which gaps in the transmission medium usage are an important component of the coordination process that divides up access to the medium among many stations. An important component of the 802.11ac standard is the way that a BSSID can switch channel bandwidth dynamically on a frame-by-frame basis. In any given collection of devices, it is easy to see how some might be line-powered devices without power-saving requirements and demanding the highest possible throughput, while others are battery-operated devices where battery life is at a premium. Rather than enforcing a one-bandwidth-fits-all approach, 802.11ac allows channel bandwidth to be determined on a frame-by-frame basis.

 By selecting the channel bandwidth to be used on a per-frame basis, 802.11ac can more efficiently use the available spectrum. When a wide channel is available, high data rates are possible. When only a narrow channel is available, 802.11ac can fall back to lower rates.

To help with dividing up airtime between channels, 802.11ac introduces the terminology of *primary* and *secondary* (or, more formally, *non-primary*) channels. The primary channel is the channel used to transmit something at its native bandwidth. Figure 3-5 is an illustration of the concept in the lowest eight available channels. For each channel bandwidth, there is one primary channel, meaning that it is the channel used to transmit frames at that channel width. This network will transmit 20 MHz frames on channel 60. To transmit a 40 MHz frame on its 40 MHz primary channel, both channels 60 and 64 must be free. To transmit an 80 MHz frame, the four channels 52 through 64 must all be free. Finally, to transmit a 160 MHz frame, all eight channels from 36 through 64 must be free. Table 3-2 shows the primary and secondary channels for each bandwidth. In practice, 802.11ac can share spectrum much more efficiently than 802.11n because detection of networks on non-primary channels is significantly better with 802.11ac hardware.

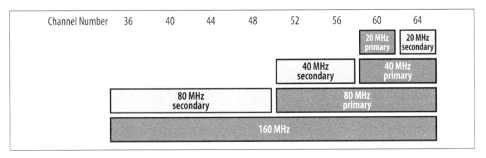

Figure 3-5. Primary and secondary channel nomenclature

Table 3-2. Primary and secondary channel relationships in Figure 3-5

Channel bandwidth	Primary channel	Secondary channel	Total number of 20 MHz channels
20 MHz	60	64	One (60)
40 MHz	60	52	Two (60, 64)
80 MHz	52	36	Four (52, 56, 60, and 64)
160 MHz	36	n/a	Eight (36, 40, 44, 48, 52, 56, 60, and 64)

One of the reasons for the notion of primary and secondary channels is that it helps multiple networks to share the same frequency space. Due to the wide variety of devices and data rates in use, a network that is designed for peak speed using 160 MHz channels will not always need the full capacity of the channel. Two networks, such as those shown in Figure 3-6, may share the same 160 MHz channel. They may both transmit 80 MHz frames at the same time because their primary 80 MHz channels are different.

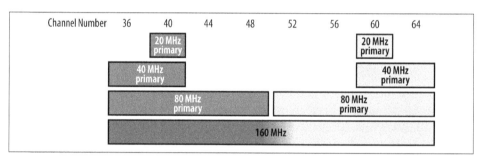

Figure 3-6. Coexistence of multiple networks in the same frequency space

The ability to share wider channels as shown in Figure 3-6 depends on the ability of an 802.11ac device to detect transmissions not only on its primary channel but also on any secondary channels in use. 802.11n's clear-channel assessment (CCA) capabilities on secondary channels were limited, and thus deploying two 802.11n networks that overlapped required in practice that the primary channels be identical. 802.11ac has sufficiently good secondary-channel CCA capabilities that two networks can readily be deployed without overlap, leading to gains for the whole network because a much larger fraction of transmissions can be done in parallel. This single subtlety in the specification allows for a wide range of deployment options for 802.11ac networks.

What Happened to the RIFS?

802.11n introduced the Reduced Interframe Space (RIFS), a shortened gap between frames that was used to improve efficiency. HT devices were allowed to separate two frames with the RIFS (2 μs) instead of the much longer SIFS (10 μs in the 2.4 GHz band and 16 μs in the 5 GHz band). If there are multiple frames to transmit to a device, however, it is much more efficient to use aggregate frames. Even with the savings from using the RIFS, transmitting two frames separately still requires two full headers and two PLCP frames. A single A-MPDU can transmit two frames at once, then receive a single block ACK. As a result, the RIFS is not used by 802.11ac.

Basic channel access rules

The most basic channel access rule is that a frame can be transmitted if the medium is idle. Whether the medium is idle depends on how wide a channel the transmission is using. Once the relevant channel has been determined to be idle, a VHT device may:

- Transmit a 20 MHz frame on its primary 20 MHz channel. Clear-channel assessment looks only at the primary 20 MHz channel.

- Transmit a 40 MHz frame on its primary 40 MHz channel. Naturally, this requires that the secondary 20 MHz channel is also idle and has passed the CCA check.

- Transmit an 80 MHz frame on its primary 80 MHz channel. As you might expect at this point, this requires that both the primary 40 MHz channel and the secondary 40 MHz channel are idle.

- Transmit a 160 MHz frame on the 160 MHz channel, but only if both the primary and secondary 80 MHz channels are idle.

If any of the necessary channels are not idle, the device must report that the channel is busy and use the backoff procedure to reacquire the channel. With the backoff procedure, the transmitter will wait until the medium is idle, allow the distributed interframe space (DIFS) to elapse, and then attempt retransmission. As part of the retransmission, the device will select a random number to use as the slot number within the contention window. In most cases, the "winner" of a retransmission attempt during contention will be the station that selects the lowest backoff number.[6]

---

6. For more information on the channel acquisition procedure, see Chapter 3 of *802.11 Wireless Networks: The Definitive Guide*.

Sensitivity requirements

To report that the channel is busy, 802.11 has two methods: *signal detection* and *energy detection*. Signal detection requires that a receiver find, lock onto, and begin decoding an 802.11-compatible signal. The second method, energy detection, looks only at the raw energy received in the band: if it is sufficiently high, the channel is reported as busy. 802.11ac keeps the same rules for CCA sensitivity for 20 MHz and 40 MHz channels that were first adopted in 802.11n, and adds rules for the new wider channels. Table 3-3 summarizes both the signal thresholds and the energy thresholds for primary and secondary channels. Two rules guide the development of these thresholds. First, every time the channel bandwidth doubles, the required signal threshold also doubles (+3 dB is a doubling of power). Second, the rule for energy detection is that on a non-primary channel, energy of 20 dB over the minimum sensitivity indicates that a channel will be busy because that is likely to be sufficient power to have an intelligible signal over the background noise.

Table 3-3. CCA sensitivity thresholds

Channel width	Signal threshold (primary)	Signal threshold (non-primary)	Energy threshold (non-primary)
20 MHz	−82 dBm	−72 dBm	−62 dBm
40 MHz	−79	−72	−59
80 MHz	−76	−69	−56
160 MHz	−73	n/a[a]	n/a[a]

[a] With 160 MHz channels, there are no secondary channels, so these thresholds are not defined.

Protection and Coexistence of 802.11ac with Older 802.11 Devices

For the designers of 802.11ac, ensuring compatibility with existing 802.11 equipment was a key requirement to meet in developing the new specification. But because of the evolutionary nature of the VHT PHY, no new protection mechanisms are required. Reuse of the OFDM PHY's physical layer header ensures that any 5 GHz device will be able to detect VHT transmissions and identify that the medium is busy.

The introduction of 802.11ac expands the compatibility matrix in the 5 GHz band from two concurrently operating technologies to three, and the compatibility considerations in a broadcast network medium extend not only to intended receivers but to any receiver. Table 3-4 describes the compatibility between transmitters of frames and their intended receivers. That is, if a transmitter of the type in the left column sends a frame directed to a receiver of the type in any of the other three columns, what will the result be? One of the major methods used to support coexistence is backward compatibility. When built, 802.11ac devices will also incorporate 802.11a and 802.11n data rates, and thus will be able to send to older peers at older data rates.

Table 3-4. Compatibility between transmitters and receivers of frames

Transmitter type	802.11a receiver	802.11n receiver	802.11ac receiver
802.11a	Designed operation	802.11n devices may receive 802.11a frames	802.11ac devices may receive 802.11a frames
802.11n	802.11n device transmits 802.11a frames (backward compatibility)	Designed operation	802.11ac devices may receive 802.11n frames
802.11ac	802.11ac device transmits 802.11a frames (backward compatibility)	802.11ac device transmits 802.11n frames (backward compatibility)	Designed operation

The more interesting side of coexistence is that any device may listen to a frame. If two 802.11ac devices are communicating with each other, how can those frames be constructed so that an older 802.11a-only device is not harmed and may still participate in sharing the network medium? By adopting the OFDM preamble, it is possible for an 802.11ac frame to be sent into the radio network and for an 802.11a device to listen to that frame's preamble, calculate the duration for which the medium will be busy, and defer transmitting to avoid collisions. Table 3-5 summarizes how various device types listening to transmissions from each of the 5 GHz PHYs will react.

Table 3-5. Compatibility between transmitters and listening devices

Transmitter type	802.11a listener	802.11n listener	802.11ac listener
802.11a	Designed operation	802.11n devices listen to 802.11a frames and defer medium access to avoid collisions	802.11ac devices listen to 802.11a frames and defer medium access to avoid collisions
802.11n	802.11n greenfield frames require RTS/CTS or CTS-to-self protection; 802.11n mixed-mode frames require no special protection	Designed operation	802.11ac devices listen to 802.11n frames and defer medium access to avoid collisions
802.11ac	802.11ac uses a compatible physical preamble, allowing 802.11a devices to read the medium as busy and avoid collisions	802.11ac uses a compatible preamble, allowing 802.11n devices to read the medium as busy and avoid collisions	Designed operation

What Happened to Greenfield Mode?

802.11n offered a "greenfield mode" that saved a few microseconds in the preamble getting a frame onto the radio link. Although it was slightly more efficient, it was not a widely adopted feature and was especially avoided in large-scale networks. The efficiency gains from greenfield mode were often lost because airtime-devouring CTS-to-self messages were required before transmitting in the greenfield mode. As a result, greenfield mode was removed from 802.11ac.

Dynamic Bandwidth Operation (RTS/CTS)

From its inception, 802.11 defined the Request to Send/Clear to Send (RTS/CTS) exchange to deal with hidden nodes. The CTS frame was later reused to provide management of the medium when transmitting to older stations. RTS and CTS frames are used only to manage access to the network medium, and they work in part because they may be transmitted at lower rates so that they may be received and understood by all stations.[7] In Figure 3-7(a), the initiator of the CTS exchange transmits the CTS at 802.11a rates, which may be understood by all recipients. All receivers of that CTS frame then know to defer access to the medium for the duration requested in the CTS, even if they are not able to receive and decode the data frame.

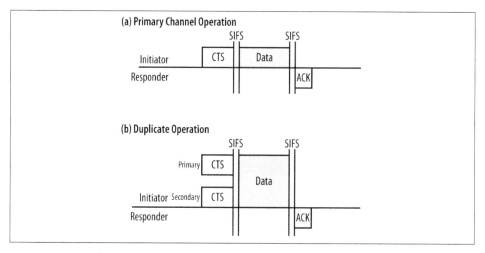

Figure 3-7. Regular and duplicate CTS frame transmission

To manage access to a wider channel, a type of transmission called a *non-HT duplicate frame* is used, which is exactly what it sounds like. Breaking it down etymologically, there are two attributes that go into non-HT duplicate transmission. First, the frame is transmitted using non-HT methods, which, practically speaking, means 802.11a transmission. Second, the frame is duplicated across multiple channels. Figure 3-7(b) shows the duplication occurring across a primary and secondary channel for a 40 MHz transmission. Wider channels may require three (80 MHz) or even seven (160 MHz) duplicate frames.

---

7. For more information on how the RTS and CTS frames use the network allocation vector to manage medium access, see *802.11 Wireless Networks: The Definitive Guide*, Chapters 4 and 14. The former chapter describes framing details and how the network allocation vector works; the latter chapter contains a detailed discussion of 802.11g protection.

Duplicate frames are used to create dynamic bandwidth signaling in 802.11ac. Even if a network is occupying, say, 80 MHz of spectrum, it will send Beacon frames and carry out access control on its primary channel. It may interact with older 802.11a stations on its primary 20 MHz channel and 802.11n stations on its primary 40 MHz channel, and only occasionally transmit frames using the full 80 MHz bandwidth. For much of the time, a network will not need its full bandwidth. Therefore, 802.11ac extended the RTS and CTS to add *bandwidth signaling*. Normally, an RTS or CTS frame only works to clear the channel on which it is transmitted. When it is used in duplicate mode to clear out multiple channels simultaneously, this is indicated by setting the Individual/Group bit in the transmitter address to 1, and the address is called a *bandwidth signaling transmitter address*.

Figure 3-8 shows how the RTS and CTS work together to negotiate the bandwidth. The initiator of a frame transmission has a frame to transmit, and would like to transmit that frame over the full 80 MHz shown in the diagram. To acquire the channel, it sends a duplicated RTS frame across all four 20 MHz channels, indicating that it would like to acquire the whole channel. In Figure 3-8(a), the receiver performs a clear-channel assessment, finds that the entire 80 MHz channel is free, and sends a CTS indicating so. As a result of the exchange, the NAV, shown in the bottom of the picture, is set on all four channels so that any other networks will defer transmission.

Figure 3-8(b) shows the dynamic bandwidth process at work. Just as in the previous scenario, the initiator begins by sending a duplicated RTS to all four 20 MHz channels in the desired 80 MHz channel. However, due to interference at the responder (say, from a colocated AP that has already taken control of two channels), it is not possible to send a CTS indicating the entire 80 MHz channel is free. Therefore, the responder sends a CTS frame on the two free channels, acquiring 40 MHz of spectrum for the transmission. With the RTS/CTS exchange complete, the initiator can send its frame using a 40 MHz transmission. Although it is a reduced channel bandwidth, the two 802.11ac devices have found and negotiated the maximum bandwidth available for transmission.

Multiple networks can use dynamic bandwidth to share access to the same wide channels. Figure 3-9(a) shows a channel map for two 802.11ac networks with primary 20 MHz channels of 56 and 60, respectively. They do not share their primary 20 MHz or 40 MHz channels, but they must share the same 80 MHz channel for transmission. If these were the only two networks installed in the same area, they could transmit 20 MHz or 40 MHz frames independently, but each would have to wait for a time when the other network was idle before using an 80 MHz channel. Figure 3-9(b) shows an example of how the network might be used over time.

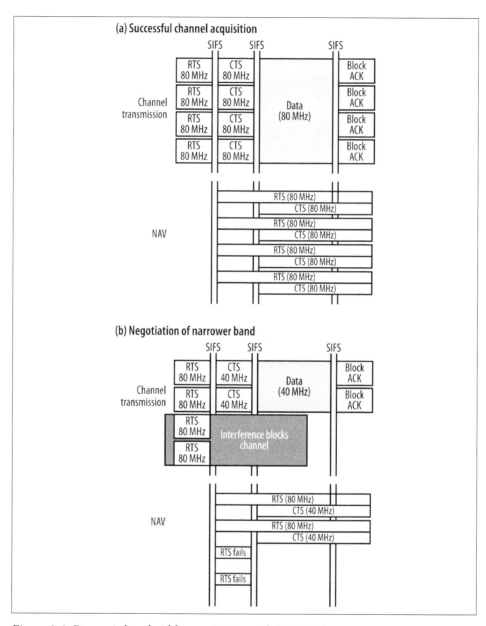

Figure 3-8. Dynamic bandwidth negotiation with RTS/CTS

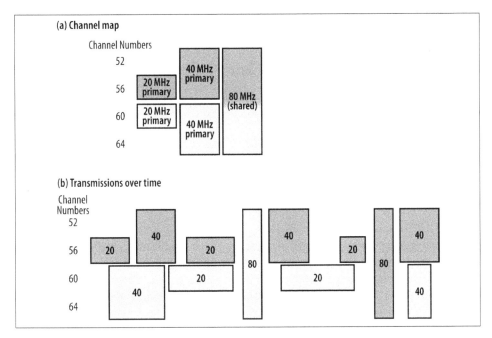

Figure 3-9. Bandwidth sharing (time dimension)

For 20 MHz and 40 MHz operation, the networks operate as independent neighbors; it is only when 80 MHz transmissions are required that the dynamic bandwidth aspect of the network comes into play. This feature in 802.11ac allows two networks to share a high-capacity 80 MHz channel without contention most of the time, which is valuable because many devices will either not be capable of 80 or 160 MHz operation, or will disable it to save battery power.

Channel Selection in 802.11ac

Per-frame selection of channel width in 802.11ac has important effects on how network administrators select channels for a network (or, alternatively, how product manufacturers design automatic channel selection protocols). Prior to 802.11ac, as long as channels were non-overlapping, there were only minor reasons to choose one versus another. An AP operating on channel 40 can easily have neighbors on channels 36 and 44 without ill effect, providing all are on 20 MHz channels. In 802.11ac, however, all three APs would share the same 80 MHz primary channel. Planning an 802.11ac network therefore involves "spreading out" primary channels to avoid overlap at the widest possible channels, a topic that we will return to in "Channel Selection" on page 118.

Security

With the adoption of the 802.11i amendment in 2004, the 802.11 working group set out the core tenets of the Robust Security Network (RSN). In particular, the Counter Mode with CBC-MAC Protocol (CCMP) has proven to be a durable cryptographic system, and has successfully protected data on wireless networks from its standardization through the adoption of 802.11n in 2009. As part of the 802.11n specification, earlier and weaker cryptographic systems were removed from use.[8] 802.11ac makes no major changes to security. CCMP remains the primary method used to protect data frames as they fly through the air at 802.11ac data rates.

At its heart, CCMP uses the Advanced Encryption Standard (AES) cipher. Knowing the cipher used is only part of the story, though, because encryption algorithms can be used in many different ways, called *modes*. Roughly speaking, a cipher mode describes how much data is encrypted in an application of the cipher and how multiple cipher blocks can be linked together to protect larger amounts of data, such as a LAN frame or TCP segment. From a security perspective, CCMP remains strong. Cryptographic systems, however, may need to be replaced for reasons other than security; of the many other reasons that may lead to the replacement of a cryptographic system, insufficient performance is common.[9]

CCMP uses AES in the *counter mode* (the first C in CCMP) and then applies a *cipher-block chained message authentication code* (CBC-MAC, the second C and the M in CCMP). Figure 3-10 shows how the system works. AES blocks are 128 bits long. To handle frames ranging in size from the shortest ARP frame to a maximum-length aggregate frame, the frames are first divided into blocks. Each block is authenticated and encrypted, with the authentication requiring one AES operation and the encryption requiring a second AES operation. Authentication uses cipher-block chaining; the "chaining" in the name refers to the way that the output from the first block is used on the second block, the output from the second block is used on the third block, and so on. Message authentication of each block depends on the previous block's operations being completed, preventing parallel operations. To encrypt, say, a standard 1,500-byte Ethernet frame requires about 200 AES operations.

---

8. TKIP and WEP cannot be used with 802.11n data rates. This prohibition extends to 802.11ac data rates because all 802.11ac devices are required to implement 802.11n protocol features. For more discussion on reasons for removing TKIP and WEP support with 802.11n, see Chapter 5 of *802.11n: A Survival Guide*.

9. For example, Triple DES is widely believed to be practically secure, but its slow speed is a serious drawback.

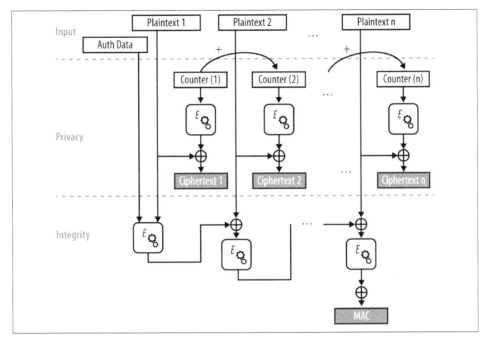

Figure 3-10. CCMP block diagram

Although CCMP has no theoretical limit to the speeds it can operate at, the use of a block-chaining mode for authenticating each block cannot be parallelized, so there is a practical performance limit placed on real-world implementations. Due to concerns about high latency in 802.11ad, that project specified the *Galois/Counter Mode Protocol* (GCMP). At a high level, GCMP is functionally similar to CCMP. A large data set, such as a wireless LAN frame, is given to the encryption layer for protection. The frame is divided into blocks, and those blocks are authenticated and encrypted. Figure 3-11 shows the system block diagram. While it looks similar, there is one important difference between the two in the authentication step. Rather than using block chaining to authenticate each data block, GCM uses a Galois field multiplication. In contrast to block chains that require each block to be processed before moving on to the next one, Galois field multiplications can be run in parallel. In addition, Galois multiplications are less computationally intensive than the cipher block encryption algorithms required by a CBC-MAC.[10] By transferring the work of authenticating the frame from the block cipher

---

10. Both Intel and AMD now include instructions for Galois field multiplication in microprocessors. The Carry-less Multiplication (CLMUL) instruction set on Intel's Westmere, Sandy Bridge, and Ivy Bridge chips and AMD's Bulldozer and Piledriver can be applied to perform the Galois field multiplication. An Intel application note specifically describes how to use these instructions for support of GCM: *http://software.intel.com/en-us/articles/intel-carry-less-multiplication-instruction-and-its-usage-for-computing-the-gcm-mode/*.

to the Galois field, GCMP also reduces the number of encryption algorithms, further increasing efficiency.

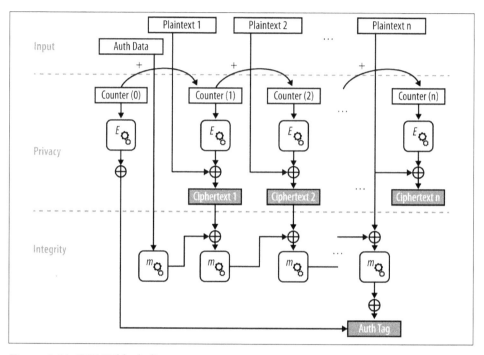

Figure 3-11. GCMP block diagram

GCM is not widely used within 802.11 wireless LANs.[11] The GCM-based cryptosystem being standardized by 802.11ad (GCMP) is not required for use with 802.11ac, but it may be used if it is present. The additional performance of GCMP will not be needed to introduce early 802.11ac products, but as speeds increase and multi-user MIMO drives up the total data rate, the efficiency of GCMP may be required. When GCMP is used in 802.11ac, it must be used for both the unicast and broadcast/multicast frames.

Mandatory MAC Features

Although 802.11ac is a complex specification, the MAC changes are comparatively simple. Table 3-6 classifies protocol features as either mandatory or optional; this chapter has concentrated on the main mandatory features.

---

11. It is, however, a common element in LAN cryptosystems. RFC 4106 describes how to apply GCM within the IPsec framework, and it was adopted by 802.1AE-2006 ("MACsec") due to its superior efficiency.

Table 3-6. Feature classification of MAC features

Feature	Mandatory/Optional	Comments
A-MPDU (receive and transmit)	Mandatory	A-MPDU operation was widely implemented in 802.11n hardware, and it is required for use with all 802.11ac devices
Single-user beamforming	Optional	Discussed in **Chapter 4**
Multi-user beamforming	Optional	Discussed in Chapter 4
CCA on secondary channels	Mandatory	
Bandwidth signaling in RTS/CTS	Mandatory to receive, optional to transmit	
GCMP	Optional	Unlikely to be required by industry certification programs

Beamforming in 802.11ac

You can't depend on your network when your
transmission is out of focus.

—Mark Twain, as network administrator

In wired networking, the biggest innovation of the last two decades was the introduction of Ethernet switching, which dramatically increased network capacity by moving from relatively large collision domains (a multi-port hub) to minimum-sized collision domains (a single port). Wireless LANs have offered great benefits to network users, primarily in the form of mobility, but in return have expanded the collision domain from an Ethernet switch port to the coverage area of an access point. Beamforming and its application in the form of multi-user MIMO in 802.11ac have the potential to change how networks are built and increase capacity well beyond the headline rate of the network equipment. In essence, multi-user MIMO works by taking advantage of beamforming to send frames to spatially diverse locations at the same time, building the first standardized version of an 802.11 "switch." Beamforming is not inherently more useful in one direction of the link, but typically enterprise access points are less resource-constrained, have access to more memory, power (both computational and electrical), and have more antennas. Therefore, beamforming in the downlink direction from the AP to the client was a ripe area for innovation in the 802.11ac standard.

Beamforming Basics

Traditionally, access points have been equipped with omnidirectional antennas, which are so named because they send energy in all directions.[1] Frequently, omnidirectional coverage will be shown as a circle on an overhead-view map, centered on the AP. Omnidirectional antennas are cheap, and more importantly, they spray radio waves in every direction, freeing the AP of the need to track each client. As long as the client is reachable in some direction, the signal from the AP will get there. Of course, the downside to that is that the radio channel is busy in all directions, as shown in Figure 4-1 by the "omnidirectional" circle.

An alternative method of transmission is to focus energy toward a receiver, a process called *beamforming*.[2] Provided the AP has sufficient information to send the radio energy preferentially in one direction, it is possible to reach farther. The overall effect is illustrated in Figure 4-1. Beamforming focuses energy toward a client, such as to the laptop computer at the right side of the figure. The wedges illustrate the areas where the beamforming focus increases power, and therefore the signal-to-noise ratio and data rates. The mirrored preferential transmission to the left is a common effect of focusing energy in a system with limited antenna elements. However, focusing the energy toward the left and right sides of the figure means that the AP's range in other directions is smaller.

Beamforming increases the performance of wireless networks at medium ranges. At short ranges, the signal power is high enough that the SNR will support the maximum data rate. At long ranges, beamforming does not offer a substantial gain over an omnidirectional antenna, and data rates will be identical to non-beamformed transmissions. Beamforming works by improving what is called the *rate over range*—at a given distance from the AP, a client device will have better performance. One way to illustrate the improved performance is shown in Figure 4-2. Range from the AP increases to the right, and the distance from the left edge of the figure is meant to roughly approximate the range of that data rate. As described previously, there is a large gap of about 5 dB between the 256-QAM rates and the next set of rates down. The lower line shows the same range data, shifted right to reflect a typical beamforming gain. At any given range, the beamformed data rate will be higher, but it is most effective at pulling in the 64-QAM rates in the middle ranges.

---

1. Omni antenna coverage is not a perfect sphere. It's usually more like a doughnut with an AP at the center and the torus spread out horizontally. Most AP coverage diagrams are drawn from the perspective of an observer looking down on the network from the top, though, so omnidirectional antennas are depicted as a having a circular coverage area.

2. Beamforming is sometimes also called *beam steering*, for obvious reasons. I prefer beam steering as a term because it describes the effects of the process better, but I have chosen to use the term preferred by the authors of the standard in this book.

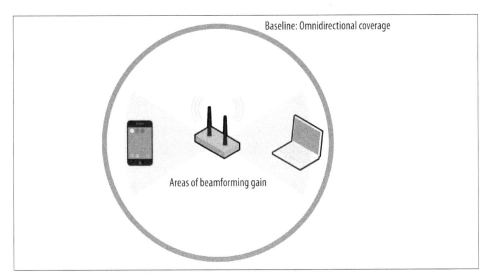

Figure 4-1. Beamforming basics

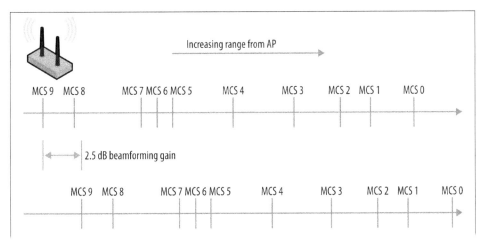

Figure 4-2. Beamforming range effects

Prior to the development of the 802.11n standard, nearly all access points on the market used antennas with static radiation patterns. APs with internal antennas were almost invariably omnidirectional, while external antennas came in a variety of different radiation patterns. Network designers could choose to use antennas with longer range and narrower beam widths, but once the antenna was selected, its coverage area was set. Beamforming uses antenna arrays to dynamically alter the transmission pattern of the AP, and the transmission pattern can be changed on a per-frame basis. Broadcast and multicast traffic is designed to be received for multiple stations, so a beamforming AP will use traditional omnidirectional transmission methods for broadcast packets to maintain coverage throughout the designed coverage area.

One analogy that I use when describing beamforming is to recall retailer John Wanamaker's statement that half of his advertising spending was wasted, but he did not know which half of his spending was unproductive. Fortunately for beamforming, it is possible to measure the channel and determine how to best use the available transmit power to reach a client device. Figure 4-3 shows a highly simplified beamforming process consisting of the major steps. In the figure, the AP is sending higher-level data such as IP packets to a laptop as the recipient. The process begins by measuring the radio channel between the two devices in a calibration process. Although in general beamforming may be either *explicit* or *implicit*, depending on whether special channel measurement frames are used, in 802.11ac the standard form of beamforming requires the use of channel measurement frames and is only explicit.

 Because 802.11ac beamforming is based on explicit channel measurements, both the transmitter and the receiver must support it.

Any device that shapes its transmitted frames is called a *beamformer*, and a receiver of such frames is called a *beamformee*. 802.11 defines new terms for the sender and receiver of beamformed frames because in a single exchange it is possible to have only one initiator and one responder, but a station may be both a beamformer and a beamformee. For example, in Figure 4-3, the AP initiates a frame exchange to the laptop. It begins by exchanging frames to measure the channel. The result of the channel measurement is a derivation of the *steering matrix*, which is a mathematical description of how to direct transmitted energy toward the receiver. Roughly speaking, it describes how to set up each element of the transmitter's antenna system to precisely overlap transmissions to reach farther.

After completing the channel measurement, the AP is capable of acting as a beamformer and sending spatially focused frames to the laptop. (Naturally, the process of sending data to the laptop may consist of setting up block acknowledgement operations and multiple aggregate frames.) At the conclusion of the data transmission, the laptop must, as required by 802.11 protocol rules, positively acknowledge receipt of the data. This acknowledgement may be beamformed as well, in which case the laptop will also act as a beamformer for the transmission of acknowledgements. In a frame exchange between two devices, either side may choose to calibrate the channel for beamforming purposes;

when client devices have large amounts of data to transmit, the standard allows them to calibrate the channel to steer transmissions toward their serving AP.[3]

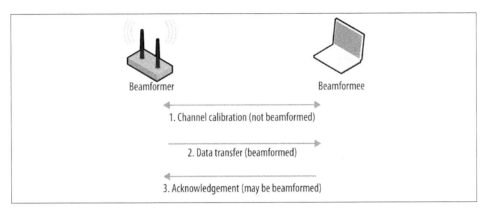

Figure 4-3. Beamforming terminology and process

To steer transmissions in a particular direction, a beamformer will subtly alter what is transmitted by each array. As an example, Figure 4-4 shows a simple phase shift. In Figure 4-4(a), all antennas transmit at the same time. As a result, the total transmission radiates in each direction equally. In the figure, this is illustrated by showing that the transmissions from each individual array element go out at the same speed at the same time, and therefore cover the same distance. In Figure 4-4(b), the array applies a phase shift to each element so that the element on the right transmits first and the element on the left transmits last. As a result, the transmissions from the array will converge along a different path that is shifted to the left. The steering matrix is a precise mathematical description of how the antenna array should use each individual element to select a spatial path for the transmission. 802.11ac beamforming is significantly more complicated than is illustrated by this example, however, because beamforming operates on pairwise relationships between the beamformer and the beamformee.

Gains from beamforming are variable and depend on the radio environment, the sophistication of the antenna array on both sides of the link, the relative motion of both sides of the link, and many other factors. Like many features in 802.11ac, beamforming results in a modest improvement in the performance of the underlying protocol, and it must be used with many other techniques to see dramatic performance improvements. A reasonable expectation would be that beamforming can result in a gain of anywhere between 2 to 5 dB, with the best results coming for mid-range transmissions. At short

---

3. In practice, beamforming is easier to do in the "downstream" (AP to client) direction because APs have more sophisticated antenna arrays.

ranges, transmissions are already at the maximum data rate and there will not be any gain in speed. At long ranges, the beamforming gain is not sufficient to add speed.

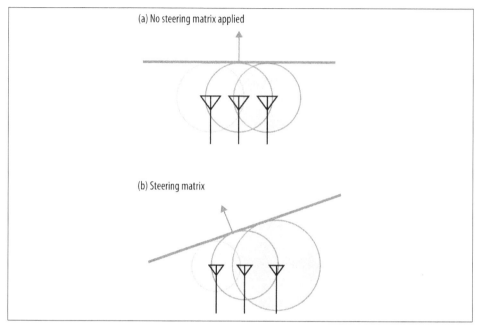

Figure 4-4. Using multiple antennas to steer transmissions

 Beamforming gains are expected to be approximately 3 dB in the transmitted direction. In practice, this gain will typically be one step up in data rates (increasing one MCS number) for a mid-range transmission.

Transmit Power Limitations and Beamforming

802.11ac operates subject to regulations regarding transmit power. When MIMO was first introduced, regulators imposed a limit based on the *array gain*. MIMO systems improve performance by analyzing signals across multiple antennas, which offers a signal-processing gain that is equivalent in concept to simply using a larger antenna. The array gain is related to the number of antennas in the array and is defined as 10*log(N), where N is the number of antennas in the array. For a two-antenna system the array gain is 3 dB, and for a three-antenna system the array gain is 4.8 dB.

Regulatory rules are typically a cap on effective radiated power (ERP), and ERP includes the array gain in both the US and Europe. Because ERP is the sum of the power from the Wi-Fi radio itself plus the antenna gain, in practice, regulations impose a lower limit on MIMO systems. For a two-antenna MIMO array limited to 20 dBm ERP, the maximum input power to the array will be 17 dBm because the ERP includes the array gain: 17 dBm conducted power + 3 dB antenna gain = 20 dBm ERP. European regulations have always required that the array gain adjustment be used only in "correlated" transmission methods such as beamforming; rules in the US required the array gain adjustment to all transmissions until October 2012. As this book went to press, transmit beamforming implementations were required to use a lower radio power output than other forms of MIMO.[4] This may limit the practical advantage of transmit beamforming systems, at least until regulatory rules are changed again.

Null Data Packet (NDP) Beamforming in 802.11ac

One of the biggest changes between 802.11n and 802.11ac is that beamforming has been dramatically simplified. Proprietary beamforming technologies had existed prior to 802.11n, but it was only in 802.11n that a standard for beamforming was introduced. In the 802.11n specification, multiple beamforming methods were described. Before using beamforming, both sides of the link had to agree on one method they shared, but due to the complexity of implementing multiple methods, many product vendors chose not to implement any. To avoid a repeat with 802.11ac, engineers writing the specification settled on just one method of beamforming, called *null data packet (NDP) sounding*. The second major change in beamforming with 802.11ac has not yet been realized, but it has the potential to dramatically change how much data wireless networks can support. 802.11ac's second wave of products will introduce multi-user MIMO, an application of MIMO techniques that allows simultaneous transmission to multiple clients.

Channel measurement (sounding) procedures

Beamforming depends on channel calibration procedures, called *channel sounding* in the 802.11ac standard, to determine how to radiate energy in a preferred direction. Many factors may influence how to steer a beam in a particular direction. Within the multi-carrier OFDM channel used by 802.11ac, there may be a strong frequency-dependent response that requires limiting data rates over the channel. Alternatively, between two 802.11ac devices, a particular frequency may respond much more strongly to one path than another. Beamforming enables the endpoints at either side of a link to get maximum performance by taking advantage of channels that have strong

---

4. For more information, see my blog post at *http://blogs.aerohive.com/blog/the-wi-fi-security-blog/did-the-fcc-really-limit-80211ac-beamforming.*

performance while avoiding paths and carriers that have weak performance.[5] Mathematically, the ability to steer energy is represented by the *steering matrix*, which is given the letter Q in 802.11ac. Matrices are used to represent steering information because they are an excellent tool for representing the frequency response from each transmission chain in the array over each transmission stream. Matrix operations allow the spatial mapper to alter the signal to be transmitted for each OFDM subcarrier over each path to the receiver in one operation. Naturally, after applying the steering matrix to the data for transmission, it will leave the antenna array in a decidedly non-omnidirectional pattern.

Channel sounding consists of three major steps:

1. The beamformer begins the process by transmitting a Null Data Packet Announcement frame, which is used to gain control of the channel and identify beamformees. Beamformees will respond to the NDP Announcement, while all other stations will simply defer channel access until the sounding sequence is complete.

2. The beamformer follows the NDP Announcement with a null data packet. The value of an NDP is that the receiver can analyze the OFDM training fields to calculate the channel response, and therefore the steering matrix. For multi-user transmissions, multiple NDPs may be transmitted.

3. The beamformee analyzes the training fields in the received NDP and calculates a feedback matrix. The feedback matrix, referred to by the letter V in the 802.11ac specification, enables the beamformer to calculate the steering matrix.

4. The beamformer receives the feedback matrix and calculates the steering matrix to direct transmissions toward the beamformee.

With the steering matrix in hand, the beamformer can then transmit frames biased in a particular direction, as shown in Figure 4-5. Without beamforming, energy is radiated in all directions more or less equally. Along any direction away from the beamformer, the signal level will be roughly comparable (assuming an ideal omnidirectional antenna). If the transmitter applies a steering matrix, however, the array will send energy in a way that prefers one path. On the preferred path, transmissions from the array will reinforce each other and become stronger, and on other paths, the transmissions from the array will interfere with each other and become weaker. In effect, the combination of the steering matrix and the channel determines whether a signal becomes stronger or weaker.

---

5. One subtle distinction between 802.11n and 802.11ac is that the latter does away with the unequal modulation (UEQM) modes. UEQM was originally standardized because one effect of beamforming may be to emphasize that certain carriers or paths are less able to sustain high data rates, due to frequency-specific effects. One of the reasons why UEQM was never widely deployed with 802.11n is that very few 802.11n implementations ever made use of explicit beamforming.

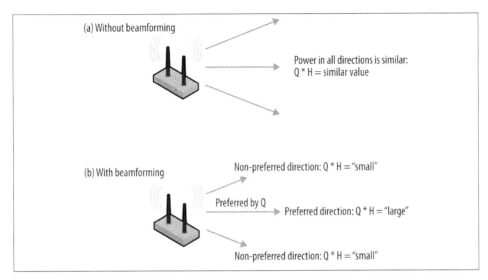

Figure 4-5. Effects of steering matrix

Channel sounding procedures do have a cost in airtime because the sounding exchange must complete before a beamformed transmission can be sent. If the speed gain from transmitting a beamformed frame is not sufficient to offset the airtime consumed by the sounding exchange, the overall speed will be slower. Roughly speaking, a sounding exchange requires 500 microseconds.[6] Once the effect of contention is added into the mix, a rough guideline is that the sounding procedure requires about 0.5% to 1% of available airtime, which can add up to a substantial fraction of available capacity on networks with high numbers of clients.

The feedback matrix

The key to beamforming is calculating the steering matrix Q for the channel between the beamformer and the beamformee. The steering matrix can potentially have quite large dimensions because it represents the channel behavior between each of the transmitters in the beamformer's array and each of the receivers in the beamformee's array. Rather than transmitting a steering matrix, the beamformee calculates a feedback matrix and compresses it so that it can be represented by a smaller frame and thus take up less airtime. Compression of the beamforming matrix is accomplished by using matrix

---

6. Timing for a sounding exchange is determined mainly by the size of the feedback matrix. Both the NDP Announcement and the NDP are fairly short. After gaining control of the channel, the NDPA and NDP frames require about 100 microseconds. For computing the duration required for the feedback matrix, it's necessary to make an assumption about the achievable data rate, which is itself a function of the channel bandwidth and modulation and coding. To get to a rough figure of 500 microseconds, I assumed that the channel was able to support a data rate at the lower end of the middle range of data rates.

operations to send a representative set of values that can be used to reconstitute the matrix instead of sending the raw matrix itself.

To calculate the feedback matrix, the beamformee runs through the following procedure:[7]

1. Calculating the feedback matrix can only begin after receiving the NDP from the beamformer. Once the NDP is received, each OFDM subcarrier is processed independently in its own matrix that describes the performance of the subcarrier between each transmitter antenna element and each receiver antenna element. The contents of the matrix are based on the received power and phase shifts between each pair of antennas.

2. The feedback matrix is transformed by a matrix multiplication operation called a Givens rotation, which depends on parameters called "angles." Rather than transmitting the full feedback matrix, the beamformee calculates the angles based on the matrix rotation. The 802.11ac standard specifies the order in which these angles are transmitted so that the beamformer can receive a long string of bits and appropriately delimit each angle.

3. Having calculated the angles, the beamformee assembles them into the compressed feedback form and returns them to the beamformer. Only one set of angles is required to summarize the radio link performance for all of the OFDM subcarriers, though naturally, the set of angles can be quite large with wider channels.

4. The beamformer receives the feedback matrix and uses it to calculate the steering matrix for transmissions to the beamformee.

One feedback matrix is sent by each beamformee. In single-user beamforming, there is one feedback matrix from the beamformee and one steering matrix used. In multi-user beamforming, each beamformee sends a feedback matrix and the beamformer must maintain a steering matrix for each client.

When transmitting the feedback matrix, there are three main factors that determine its size. First, wider channels have more OFDM subcarriers, so the feedback matrix must be larger to accommodate them. Second, the higher the number of pairwise combinations of transmitter and receiver antennas is, the larger the matrix will be. Finally, 802.11ac allows two different representations of the angle values to enable devices to use higher resolution when necessary. The relevant sizes are summarized in Table 4-1. Multi-user MIMO requires higher resolution because of the need to avoid inter-user interference, a problem unique to multi-user transmissions.

---

7. Feedback matrix calculations are not for the faint of heart. 802.11ac borrows heavily from the beamforming procedures first established in 802.11n. If you want the gory details of the matrix math used to calculate the feedback matrix, see clause 20.3.12.3 in 802.11-2012, and read up on Givens rotations, which are named after the scientist at the Argonne National Laboratory who invented them.

Table 4-1. Parameters of the feedback matrix V

Number of subcarriers[a]	Per-subcarrier angle count[b]	Angle field size
20 MHz channel: 52 subcarriers	2x2: 2 angles/subcarrier	Single-user: 6 bits or 10 bits/angle
40 MHz channel: 108 subcarriers	3x3: 6 angles/subcarrier	Multi-user: 12 bits or 16 bits/angle
80 MHz channel: 234 subcarriers	4x4: 12 angles/subcarrier	
160 MHz channel: 486 subcarriers	6x6: 30 angles/subcarrier	
	8x8: 56 angles/subcarrier	

[a] Subcarriers can be grouped to reduce the report size.

[b] Many combinations of size for the beamforming matrix are available. This table shows the maximum number of angles because it focuses on symmetric systems, but combinations are available for any number of transmitters from 2 through 8, and any number of receivers up to the number of transmitters.

To estimate the size of the feedback matrix, multiply the results of each of the three columns in Table 4-1:

Single-user 2x2 MIMO @ 20 MHz, low resolution: 78-byte report
52 subcarriers x 2 angles/subcarrier x 6 bits/angle = 624 bits or 78 bytes. This is the smallest steering matrix available in 802.11ac.

Single-user 3x3 MIMO @ 80 MHz, high resolution: 1.7 kB report
234 subcarriers x 6 angles/subcarrier x 10 bits/angle = 14,040 bits or 1.7 kB. This will be a typical steering matrix for a single-user MIMO system released in the first wave of 802.11ac.

Single-user 4x4 MIMO @ 80 MHz, high resolution: 3.4 kB report
This is the same as the previous example, but it adds an additional transmitter and receiver. In a 4x4 system there are more degrees of freedom, which is why there are more angles required per subcarrier.

Multi-user 8x8 MIMO @ 80 MHz, high resolution: 53 kB report
486 subcarriers x 56 angles/subcarrier x 16 bits/angle = 435,456 bits or 53 kB. Large sets of angles can group subcarriers together in order to reduce the report size and help it fit into a frame. In practice, a multi-user report with 80 MHz channels would group subcarriers to reduce the report size.

Single-User (SU) Beamforming

Single-user beamforming is readily understandable because its purpose is to shape a transmission from a single transmitter to a single receiver. As shown in Figure 4-6, the beamformer sends a null data packet, which is a frame with a known fixed format. By analyzing the received NDP frame, the beamformee calculates a *feedback matrix* that is sent in a reply frame. Beamformees do not send a steering matrix directly because the beamforming sounding protocol needs to enable multiple-user MIMO, as described in the next section.

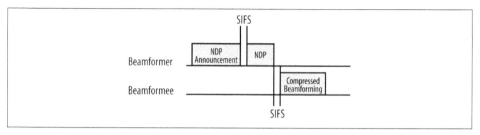

Figure 4-6. Single-user channel calibration procedure

Channel Calibration for Single-User Beamforming

The channel calibration procedure is carried out as a single operation, in which the beamformer and beamformee cooperatively measure the channel to provide the raw data needed to calculate the steering matrix. The sounding procedure does not transmit the steering matrix directly, but instead works to exchange all the information necessary for the beamformer to calculate its own steering matrix.

NDP Announcement frame

The channel sounding process begins when the beamformer transmits a Null Data Packet Announcement frame, which is a control frame and is depicted in Figure 4-7. The entire channel sounding process is carried out in one burst, so the duration set in an NDP Announcement corresponds to the length of the full exchange of three frames. In single-user MIMO beamforming, the NDP Announcement frame relays the size of the feedback matrix by identifying the number of columns in the feedback matrix.

The main purpose of the NDP Announcement frame is to carry a single STA Info field for the intended beamformee. The STA Info field is two bytes long and consists of three fields:

AID12 (12 least significant bits of the intended beamformee's association ID)
Upon association to an 802.11 access point, client devices are assigned an association ID. The least significant 12 bits of the beamformee's association ID are included in this field. When a client device acts as a beamformer, this field is set to 0 because the AP does not have an association ID.

Feedback Type
In a single-user NDP Announcement frame, this field is always 0.

Nc Index

This index describes the number of columns in the feedback matrix, with one column for each spatial stream. As a three-bit field it can take on eight values, which matches the eight streams supported by 802.11ac. This field is set to the number of spatial streams minus one.

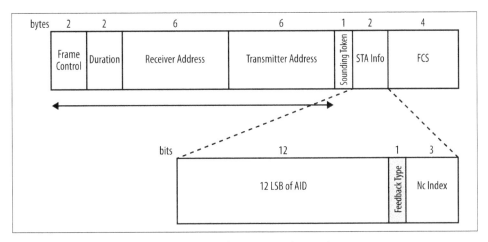

Figure 4-7. NDP Announcement frame format (single-user)

NDP frame

Upon transmission of the NDP Announcement frame, the beamformer next transmits a Null Data Packet frame, which is shown in Figure 4-8. The reason for the name "null data packet" should be obvious in looking at the frame; Figure 4-8 shows a PLCP frame with no data field, so there is no 802.11 MAC frame. Channel sounding can be carried out by analyzing the received training symbols in the PLCP header, so no MAC data is required in an NDP. Within an NDP there is one VHT Long Training Field (VHT-LTF) for each spatial stream used in transmission, and hence in the beamformed data transmission.

Figure 4-8. NDP format

VHT Compressed Beamforming Action frame

Following receipt of the NDP, the beamformee responds with a feedback matrix. The feedback matrix tells the beamformer how the training symbols in the NDP were received, and therefore how the beamformer should steer the frame to the beamformee.

Figure 4-9 shows the format of the compressed beamforming report frame used in single-user MIMO. The Action frame header indicates that the frame contains a feedback matrix.

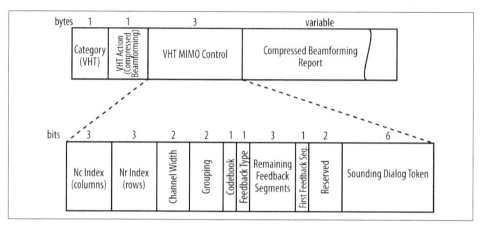

Figure 4-9. Compressed Beamforming Action frame (single-user)

The VHT MIMO Control field, included next, enables a beamformer to interpret the feedback matrix by describing the following attributes:

Size of the feedback matrix (6 bits)

The Nc Index and Nr Index fields describe the size of the feedback matrix in terms of the number of columns and the number of rows. When using beamformed transmissions over large numbers of spatial streams, the matrix will be quite large.

Channel width (2 bits)

The feedback matrix's size also depends on the size of the underlying channel. Wider channels require larger feedback matrices because there are more individual carriers to measure.

Grouping (2 bits)

When parts of the beamforming matrix are repeated, the beamformee can group multiple spatial streams together to reduce the size of the transmitted matrix.

Codebook (1 bit)

Roughly speaking, a beamforming matrix is used to describe the phase shifts required by each antenna element (see Figure 4-4). 802.11ac transmits the information on these angles as a long string of bits; the receiver of a steering matrix needs to know where to split the bit field into individual matrix elements, and this field is used to describe the representation of the data.

Type of feedback (1 bit)

Obviously, in single-user MIMO, the feedback type will be single user.

Flow control (10 bits)

The Remaining Feedback Segments and First Feedback Segment fields are used together with the Sounding Dialog Token to match the response from the beamformee to the beamformer's request. In very large matrices with wide bandwidths and high numbers of spatial streams, the matrix will be quite large and therefore may need to be sent to the beamformer in multiple steps.

Heisenberg Beamforming: Single-User and Multi-User Beamforming Compared

Now that two types of beamforming are possible in 802.11, the inevitable question is how they compare. They both take advantage of an antenna array to steer energy toward a client device, so they are superficially similar. They both operate in the same environment of an AP surrounded by clients, and both improve the signal-to-noise ratio.

Multi-user beamforming, however, introduces a time dimension to the transmission process. Experience with single-user beamforming shows that a channel measurement is good for approximately a tenth of a second. At least, for the purpose of gross estimation, a tenth of a second is the right order of magnitude; sounding measurements clearly are not good for a whole second, but they are useful for well more than a hundredth of a second. Even though a tenth of a second is barely any time for the human user of the computing device, it does not allow much time for the channel to change. At walking speed, a tenth of a second will result in a movement of about 6 inches (17 cm). In single-user beamforming, the channel is still being used by only one transmitter and one receiver, so there will not be substantial changes to the performance of the channel in this period.

Multi-user beamforming, on the other hand, is significantly more time-dependent. At a given instant, the multi-user transmitter will be sending frames to more than one receiver. To correctly shape those transmissions, the beamformer will need to have up-to-date channel information on the entire channel, which requires fresh measurement data for each beamformee. Unlike single-user beamforming, in which the channel can be completely understood by performing one set of measurements, multi-user beamforming requires updating the channel measurements each time the spatial arrangement of receivers changes.

Multi-user beamforming channel measurements must therefore work like a strobe light, measuring the channel often enough that each "flash" (channel measurement) is able to "freeze" the relative positions of the beamformees. Although commercial multi-user beamforming is not yet available, a good rule of thumb is that channel measurement must occur on significantly shorter time scales to be effective—probably along the lines of 10 ms instead of the 100 ms that is acceptable in single-user beamforming. At such a short time scale, devices carried at walking speed will be able to move less than an inch (about 1.75 cm) between measurements.

Multi-User (MU) Beamforming

By simplifying beamforming to use one method of channel sounding, 802.11ac will enable wider use of standards-based beamforming. More significant, however, is the inclusion of multi-user (MU) MIMO beamforming in 802.11ac. Prior to the introduction of multi-user beamforming, all 802.11 devices could send a transmission to only one device at a time. Just as Ethernet switches reduced the scope for collisions from a large network down to a single port, multi-user MIMO reduces the spatial collision domain. By using MU-MIMO, an AP may transmit to multiple receiving stations simultaneously.

 Due to the need for sophisticated antenna systems and signal processing, MU-MIMO in 802.11ac can be used only in the downstream direction, from an AP to multiple client devices.

One important capability that MU-MIMO brings to 802.11ac is its support of single-stream devices. Prior to 802.11ac, beamforming worked to increase the signal-to-noise ratio of a link to a single device, but the devices on the network often limited its benefits. Many small battery-powered devices are capable of only a single spatial stream, and thus receive only limited benefits from single-user MIMO. With 802.11ac's multi-user MIMO, a single transmission time can be used to send frames to multiple single-stream receivers. The 802.11ac standard allows up to four different receiver groups within one MU-MIMO transmission.

 Multi-user MIMO can transmit simultaneously to multiple single-stream devices, which enables the network to more efficiently serve increasingly common battery-powered devices such as phones and tablets.

Channel Calibration for Multi-User Beamforming

To support multi-user MIMO beamforming, 802.11ac uses an extended version of the channel sounding exchange. As shown in Figure 4-10, the multi-user channel sounding procedure requires a response from all beamformees. Each beamformee contributes information in a feedback matrix, and the beamformer uses multiple feedback matrices to produce one steering matrix.

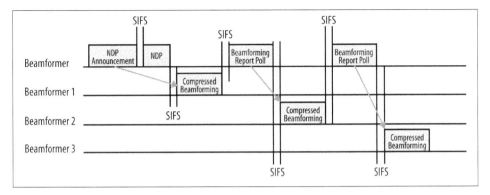

Figure 4-10. Multi-user channel sounding procedure

In Figure 4-10, the sounding procedure starts off exactly as it did in the single-user case, with an NDP Announcement and NDP that put the transmission out to begin the calibration. However, to retrieve the feedback matrix from each beamformee, the multi-user sounding procedure needs a new frame, the Beamforming Report Poll frame, to ensure that responses from all beamformees are collected. Figure 4-10 shows three beamformees, and therefore the beamformer must use two poll frames to obtain the feedback matrices from the second and third beamformees. (No poll frame is required for the first station named in the NDP Announcement frame, but the second and subsequent beamformees must be polled.) After receiving multiple responses, the beamformer will integrate all the responses together into a master steering matrix.

NDP Announcement frame

As in the single-user case, the channel sounding procedure is started by transmission of an NDP Announcement frame. The format of the NDP Announcement frame in the multi-user case is similar to the single-user NDP Announcement, with one important change. As shown in Figure 4-11, a multi-user NDP Announcement frame includes multiple Station Information records, one for each beamformee. In the Station Information fields, the NDP Announcement frame is used to request multi-user feedback as well. When an NDP Announcement is sent to multiple receivers, as it is when starting the MU-MIMO sounding process, the receiver address is the broadcast address.

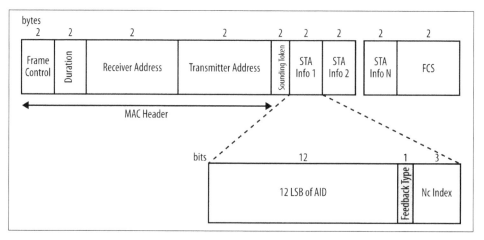

Figure 4-11. NDP Announcement frame format (multi-user)

NDP frame

Upon transmission of the NDP Announcement frame, the beamformer next transmits a Null Data Packet frame. Like NDP Announcements, null data packets are sent in single-user mode. Therefore, even in multi-user MIMO sounding, the format will be identical to the single-user format shown in Figure 4-8. A single null data packet has no MAC header information and will be received by all devices. Each device can use the received training frames in the null data packet to calculate its feedback matrix.

Compressed Beamforming Action frame

The Compressed Beamforming Action frame serves the same purpose in multi-user MIMO as it does in single-user MIMO. However, the multi-user format of the frame includes an extra field, the Multi-User Exclusive Beamforming Report field, at the end of the frame. This field carries signal-to-noise ratio differences between subcarriers and is needed to update the steering matrix when there are multiple recipients. Both report fields shown in Figure 4-12 are indicated as variable because their size depends on the number of spatial streams as well as the channel bandwidth.

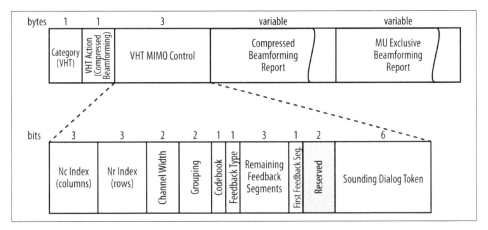

Figure 4-12. Compressed Beamforming Action frame (multi-user)

Beamforming Report Poll frame

To retrieve additional feedback from the second and subsequent beamformees, the beamformer must use the Beamforming Report Poll frame, which is a control frame. This frame is quite simple, as can be seen in Figure 4-13: it is essentially a one-byte field of retransmission requests. Each bit in the Feedback Bitmap field requests one feedback segment to be retransmitted.

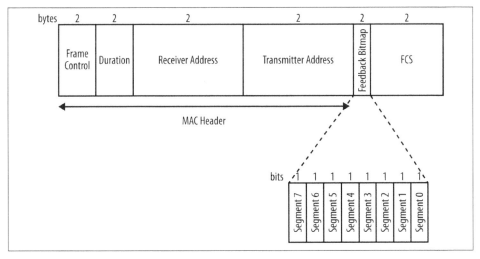

Figure 4-13. Beamforming Report Poll frame (multi-user)

Multi-User MIMO Transmission

Once the multi-user channel sounding is complete, an AP can proceed to send a multi-user transmission. Each beamformee in a multi-user transmission is called, not surprisingly, a *user*. 802.11ac supports sending up to four multi-user MIMO transmissions at one time, and the 802.11ac MAC protocol includes ways to negotiate the capabilities of each of the simultaneous transmissions. Each multi-user MIMO transmission may have a different number of spatial streams and may have its own modulation speed and coding.

 MU-MIMO transmissions are limited to four clients.

The complexity of multi-user MIMO transmission is illustrated in Figure 4-14. Just as with single-user MIMO, there are potentially multiple paths between each of the AP's antenna elements and the each of the users' antenna elements. However, there is an additional complexity to multi-user MIMO in that the number of potential paths that need to be represented in the steering matrix includes every path between each of the AP's antenna elements and every user antenna element. Each user transmission must be separately modulated.

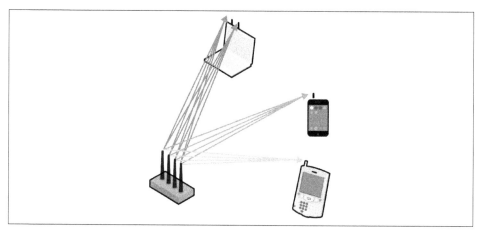

Figure 4-14. Multi-user MIMO transmission model system

To limit the system complexity, each user in an 802.11ac MU-MIMO setup is restricted to four spatial streams. 802.11ac actually supports up to eight spatial streams in the standard (though it may be some time after the initial release of 802.11ac in 2013 before hardware that implements more than four spatial streams is available). One of the trade-offs in a multi-user system is that the throughput for an individual device is lower because it can only support four streams.

MU-MIMO clients are limited to four spatial streams. If you want to go faster, you'll have to use single-user MIMO transmissions.

PHY changes for MU-MIMO

To transmit to multiple streams, a few small changes are made to the PLCP. The fields remain very similar to the descriptions in "PHY-Level Framing" on page 21, but there are a few important changes. Figure 4-15 shows the VHT Signal A field for multi-user transmissions (compare it to Figure 2-7 for the single-user format).

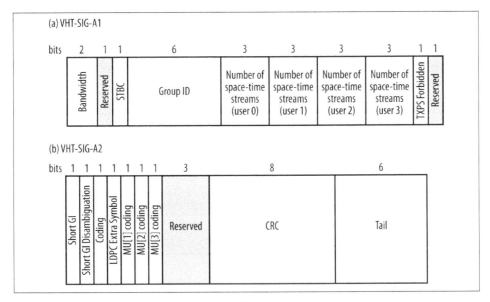

Figure 4-15. VHT-SIG-A field (multi-user format)

The changes from the single-user version of the VHT Signal A field are:

Group ID (6 bits)
> The Group ID is a protocol-layer abstraction that enables the receiver of a multi-user transmission to determine if the payload of the PLCP includes a frame sent to the receiver.

Number of space-time streams for users 0 to 3 (12 bits, 3 for each user)

A multi-user transmission may be sent to up to four simultaneous users. These sub-fields tell the recipients how many space-time streams are used for their transmissions.

Multi-user coding for users 1 to 3 (3 bits)

Where the single-user version of the VHT Signal A field holds the MCS for the payload of the PLCP, the multi-user version has bits that indicate whether convolutional coding or LDPC is used. The MCS values for each of the user streams are moved to the VHT Signal B field.

In the PLCP header, there is an OFDM-modulated header and a VHT-modulated header. In a multi-user transmission, the VHT-modulated PLCP header is available on a per-user basis, and each user has its own VHT Signal B. Figure 4-16 compares the multi-user format to the single-user format described in Chapter 2. Because the VHT Signal B field is available on a per-user basis, it includes the MCS value for the data rate. Due to the smaller number of spatial streams available to multi-user transmissions, the total number of bits devoted to the length of the individual user frames can be smaller without negative effect.

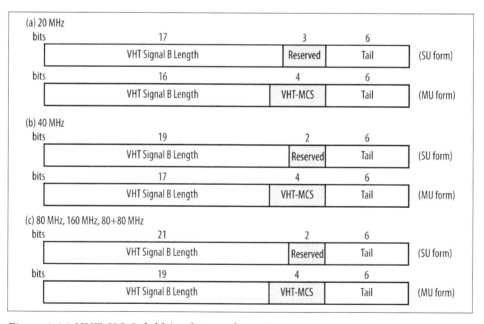

Figure 4-16. VHT-SIG-B field (multi-user format)

Transmission and reception of multi-user data streams

When transmitting a multi-user MIMO frame set, 802.11ac handles each individual user separately up to the point at which signals are combined for the analog frontend in the spatial mapper. Figure 4-17 shows a highly simplified block diagram of a two-user MIMO transmission system. Each user's input is treated independently in the digital system, where it is padded and scrambled and has forward error correction applied. Individual transmissions in a multi-user MIMO system can be coded independently, so one user may have convolutional coding and a second user may use LDPC. Each transmission is modulated at its own rate, and may or may not have STBC applied. Multiple user transmissions are only combined together in the spatial mapper, at which point the steering matrix derived from the sounding process is applied to the collective data of all users.

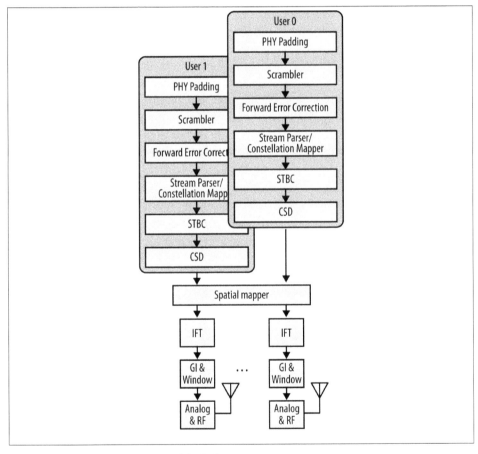

Figure 4-17. Multi-user MIMO block diagram

The most important task for a receiver of a multi-user transmission is to determine how to get at its own transmission within the multi-user stream of data while ignoring all the others. When decoding the transmissions, a receiver can process not only its own stream's VHT-modulated training fields, but also the other streams in the transmission. For obvious reasons, the other streams are called *interfering* streams. 802.11ac places no requirement on a station to decode the interfering data streams, but doing so will reduce the effects of interference.

MU-MIMO Implementation

Although it may seem like a relatively straightforward application of the MIMO technology that has been successfully applied in 802.11n for the better part of a decade, building a multi-user MIMO product has significant complexity over and above building a single-user MIMO product. One of the major limitations on MU-MIMO speeds is *inter-user interference*, which is caused by beamformees that are "too close" to each other, such that the transmission to one beamformee interferes with the transmission to another beamformee. Mitigating inter-user interference is a major hurdle for practical applications of MU-MIMO. Multi-user beamformers will likely measure the channel significantly more often to maintain up-to-date spatial location information (see the sidebar "Heisenberg Beamforming: Single-User and Multi-User Beamforming Compared" on page 73). Finally, MU-MIMO has significant effects on the queuing system in an access point. High-priority frames are still transmitted quickly, but MU-MIMO enables low-priority frames to secondary clients to be pulled forward in time.

Null steering

Inter-user interference occurs because two receivers of multi-user transmissions are not sufficiently separated. The primary goal in sending a multi-user transmission is to avoid causing this interference. Figure 4-18 illustrates the primary approach, sometimes called *null steering*. Beamforming focuses energy at a receiver, and a byproduct of this focusing effect is that outside of the intended reception area, the received signal is weaker. Multi-user MIMO transmissions combine both techniques. In the figure, there are three simultaneous transmissions. The AP has computed a steering matrix Q for each of them based on the channel measurements; the matrix H describes the effect of the channel on the transmission. In an ideal scenario, the steering matrix for each client would produce a high signal for the intended transmission, and a "null" (no reception) for the other two transmissions in the multi-user set. For example, the steering matrix for the blue client at the top of the figure would produce the frame transmitted to the blue station, but would also cancel out the transmissions to the red and green clients.

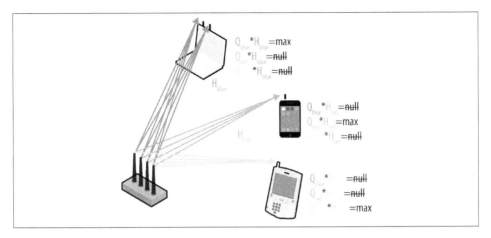

Figure 4-18. Null steering

Mathematically, effective null steering requires as many degrees of freedom as possible in the matrix. When translated into the physical world of building products, the extra degrees of freedom in the matrix are represented by additional antennas in the array. By increasing the number of antenna elements, it is possible to more accurately direct transmissions in a preferred direction and, just as importantly, ensure that the transmission is sent only in the preferred direction.

Acknowledgement in MU-MIMO

Multi-user MIMO in 802.11ac works only in the downlink direction from the AP to clients. A multi-user frame can be transmitted to multiple receivers at the same time, but the acknowledgements must be transmitted individually in the uplink direction. Every frame transmitted in 802.11ac is an aggregate frame, so 802.11ac uses the block acknowledgement procedure originally defined in 802.11n. Figure 4-19 shows one potential acknowledgement sequence for the frames transmitted by the system described in the previous section. After gaining control of the channel, the AP will transmit a multi-user frame to all receivers. In block acknowledgement, the transmitter retains control of the channel and individually requests acknowledgements where required. In the figure, the AP follows its data transmission with explicit block acknowledgement requests to each of the three receivers.

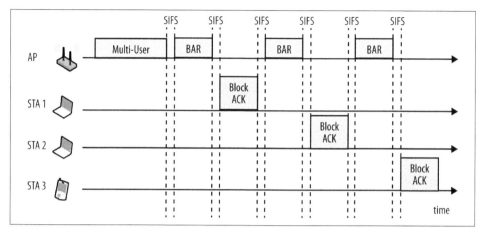

Figure 4-19. Acknowledgement in multi-user MIMO

Queuing and quality of service

Multi-user MIMO systems retain the same four queues for voice, video, best effort, and background traffic originally developed as part of the 802.11 quality of service architecture. Queuing becomes significantly more complicated with MU-MIMO, though, because a single multi-user transmission may mix high-priority frames to a priority receiver with lower-priority frames sent to a spatially distinct receiver. For example, a multi-user transmission may be scheduled to transmit voice frames to a single-stream phone and then use that transmission time to also send lower-priority data to other devices at the same time.

When an AP gains control of the channel for transmission of a multi-user transmission, it is doing so for the purpose of transmitting frames to one user. In Figure 4-14, for example, an AP may gain control of the channel in order to transmit voice frames to the phone and then choose other waiting frames for the two laptops. The access category of the traffic that drives the AP to gain control of the channel is called the *primary access category* (AC), while other access categories are called *secondary access categories*. Secondary ACs are used to support additional stations.

Figure 4-20 shows a simple example of the additional queuing required. Frames are queued from the higher protocol layers at the top of the figure, and the AP maintains four access categories for frames. In a single-user system, it is likely that frames would be transmitted from high-priority queues first, followed by lower-priority queues. In multi-user MIMO, however, frames from lower priority queues may "piggyback" onto channel access.

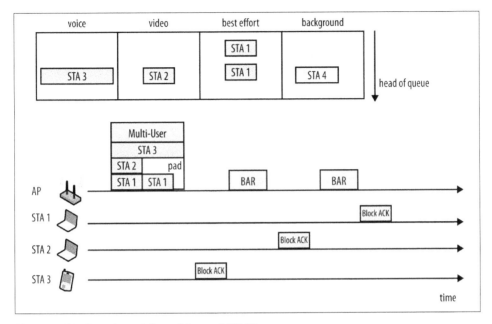

Figure 4-20. Queuing with multi-user MIMO

In this figure, there is a relatively long frame at the head of the voice queue destined for the phone. When the AP gains control of the channel to transmit the voice frame to the phone, the voice access category becomes the primary AC. The AP begins constructing a multi-user frame, and can now consider other frames and other access categories for transmission.

Frames for secondary ACs can be added into a multi-user transmission so long as they do not lengthen the overall frame. For instance, within the transmit queues in the AP it is possible to select a video frame for one laptop and two best-effort data frames for the other laptop while retaining the same overall frame transmission time, provided that the two laptop devices are located in directions that are not subject to causing inter-user interference. Even if there are other frames available, such as the background frame shown to the fourth station in Figure 4-20, they may not be included in a multi-user transmission if the receiver is not spatially distinct.

Frames on the secondary ACs gain access to the medium more quickly than they would in single-user transmission, but only because they are riding on the coattails of the frame in the primary access category. In effect, with multi-user transmission it is possible for a low-priority frame to jump the queue, provided that the low-priority frame can be transmitted simultaneously with a higher-priority non-interfering frame.

802.11ac does not specify many constraints on the design of the queuing system in an AP. Secondary ACs cannot increase the amount of airtime consumed by a multi-user packet, but given that one rule, it is possible to optimize a queuing system around many other attributes. It is acceptable to pick frames on the secondary AC that can be transmitted at the highest data rates to maximize overall throughput. Alternatively, a queuing system could be designed to transmit to the maximum number of non-overlapping receivers on secondary ACs.

CHAPTER 5

802.11ac Planning

If you don't know where you're going,
you'll end up someplace else.

—Yogi Berra

Although most of the discussion in this book has been about speed, the real value of 802.11ac to the network administrator is that it increases the capacity of a wireless network. Whether the network needs to serve more clients with today's level of throughput or today's client load with higher throughput, the solution is 802.11ac.

Several intersecting trends are driving the need for increased capacity. Many new devices are built around the assumption that 802.11 coverage is ubiquitous and therefore do not have an alternative LAN technology for accessing networks. Of these new devices, most of them are battery-operated and portable, and do not even have the capability to connect to wired Ethernet networks. As traffic shifts onto the wireless LAN, it must support new demands for connectivity. Increased numbers of devices is only the first part of a one-two punch being delivered by users. After connecting so many devices to wireless LANs, users then change the type of applications in use. With improved computing power and display technology, the user experience is becoming significantly more media-heavy, with a special emphasis on streaming multimedia and especially video support. Combine an increase in the number of devices with increased demand for capacity from each device, and you have a recipe for congestion unless greater capacity is in the cards. As the improved performance of 802.11ac becomes readily available in client devices, there will be user demand to take advantage of that speed.

Adoption of 802.11ac will likely happen more quickly than that of its predecessors. Improving speed is always welcome in networking, and many networks are built with a three- to five-year time horizon of service. Part of the planning process in building an 802.11ac network is to assess not only the current load on your network, but also the expected growth in demand for service to determine whether the increased density justifies using the highest-performance technology available. A strong industry focus on interoperability has made the transition to 802.11ac straightforward for network administrators as well.

Getting Ready for 802.11ac

802.11ac is evolutionary as much as it is revolutionary. Many of the design principles that have been used with previous technologies are still applicable, with a few minor changes to take advantage of new protocol features. The drivers to use 802.11ac are the same drivers that have justified every other network upgrade you have ever done:

Peak speed and/or throughput
> The most obvious driver for 802.11ac is the new higher speeds. Some applications require as much speed as the network can deliver, and these are obvious beneficiaries of the new technology. Increased use of video is a major driver of 802.11ac adoption, as is the increase in device density due to the widespread use of tablets and wireless LAN–equipped smartphones. Video is widely used throughout the spectrum of wireless LAN users, whether it is large and detailed images for patient care, instructional videos in the classroom, or wireless display technologies in corporate conference rooms. Higher speeds also enable additional point-to-point deployment scenarios and provide the capacity necessary to serve 802.11n clients with mesh backhaul connections.

Capacity
> With so much raw capacity, especially with wider channels, 802.11ac provides a superior level of service. In addition to the general efficiencies that the IEEE 802.11 working group builds into new specifications, products often add clever features to further extract capacity increases from the new physical layer. One common method of doing so is to bias transmissions toward frames that require shorter times to transmit. Even though 802.11ac can transmit large numbers of bits, the extremely high data rates mean that even very large amounts of data are transmitted faster than small packets were in 802.11b.

Latency
> Some applications benefit primarily from lower latency, especially real-time streaming applications such as voice, videoconferencing, or even video chat. Improving latency can be done by building a more efficient network, but often the best way to improve latency is to reduce the load on the network. 802.11 measures load by airtime utilization, so moving to faster physical layer standards improves latency by reducing the airtime load. Multi-user MIMO also has the potential to decrease network load by enabling parallel transmissions. Reducing latency means that even a few 802.11ac devices may benefit the entire network by decreasing airtime demand.

As part of the IEEE project authorization process, a task group in the formation process needs to discuss compatibility with previous technology standards. Early adopters of wireless LANs made significant investments in the technology, and the IEEE process is designed to protect that investment. Backward compatibility with prior 802.11 standards was a key consideration in the 802.11ac standardization process, and there was extensive work done in the protocol to ensure that 802.11ac would work with the many existing wireless LAN devices. In addition to physical-layer compatibility, 802.11ac has extensive MAC-layer compatibility, which enables newer 802.11ac devices to perform at their best even when surrounded by older devices. In fact, these functions were designed to enable a little bit of 802.11ac to speed up any network.

 802.11ac was designed from the beginning to be compatible with prior standards (802.11n, 802.11a/g, and 802.11b). Don't let compatibility worries slow you down—adding 802.11ac speeds up any network, even if it has only a few 802.11ac client devices.

Even though 802.11ac is the future physical layer in wireless LANs, it will not be the only physical layer. APs that are sold as "802.11ac APs" will have one 5 GHz radio running 802.11ac, and they will also have a second 2.4 GHz radio running 802.11n. Even as 802.11ac becomes established, the 2.4 GHz band will continue to depend on the same 802.11n technology that has been used for the past several years.

Catching the 802.11ac Technology Wave

Early in the development of wireless LAN technology, a new PHY was brought to market all at once. With 802.11n, however, the standards started to become much more complex, and different levels of capability came to the market in distinct "waves" or "phases." Once the basic technical details are worked out, it can often be much easier to write a standard than to build a product. For example, the work required to add four-spatial-stream support into the 802.11n standard was relatively minimal after the basic ground rules were complete, but as of the 2013 publication date of this book, four-stream 802.11n devices have yet to be brought to market because of the engineering challenges involved in building the powerful DSP required to perform the spatial mapping while staying within the 15-watt 802.3af power limit.

802.11n came to the market in waves due to the overall complexity of the standard. 802.11ac will follow this well-worn path, with a rough estimate of the contents of the first two waves in Table 5-1. The first generation of 802.11ac delivers another jump in channel bandwidth, along with a new modulation. Taken together, these two features are enough to nearly double the speed of a typical three-stream client device. The second wave of 802.11ac will add even wider channels, four-stream support, and beamforming. Although there is a temptation to focus on the headline rates only, beamforming has the potential to deliver significant gains in network capacity by improving the data rates at which most clients transmit. Not all transmissions occur at the fastest rate, so the beamforming boost can be substantial if it increases the data rates used by clients.

Table 5-1. 802.11ac technology waves

	Wave 1	Wave 2
Standard basis	802.11ac, draft 2.0	802.11ac, final version
Timeframe	Mid-2013	2014
Channel width	20, 40, and 80 MHz	Potential to add 160 MHz channels
Modulation support	Up to 256-QAM	Same as wave 1
Lowest 11ac speed	173 Mbps (20 MHz, 2-stream, 256-QAM)	Same as wave 1
Typical 11ac speed	867 Mbps (80 MHz, 2-stream, 256-QAM)	1.7 Gbps (160 MHz, 3-stream, 256-QAM)
Maximum 11ac speed	1.3 Gbps (80 MHz, 3-stream, 256-QAM)	3.5 Gbps (160 MHz, 4-stream, 256-QAM)
Beamforming	Yes (depending on underlying chipset)	Yes, possibly MU-MIMO

First wave 802.11ac versus second wave 802.11ac

A key decision in planning for 802.11ac is when to jump in and deploy widely. Unlike previous physical layers in 802.11, the first wave of 802.11ac does not offer a clear-cut compelling advantage for every user. First-wave 802.11ac products are now available, and derive their additional speed from two main protocol features. Getting the most out of the first wave of 802.11ac will require an environment that can use one or both of these features:

256-QAM
> The two top data rates in 802.11ac add 33% to the speed over 802.11n, but they require significantly higher signal-to-noise ratios. As a practical matter, such high SNRs require clean radio spectrum and short AP-to-client distances.

80 MHz channels
> Clean spectrum is required to allocate contiguous 80 MHz blocks, and even with Dynamic Frequency Selection (DFS) support, there will only be five available 80 MHz channels until the new spectrum discussed in the sidebar "Proposed Additional Spectrum for 802.11ac in the United States" on page 17 becomes available. Five channels is enough to plan a network, but it will not be as easy as it was with the multitude of channels that were available in 802.11n.

In some environments, it is possible that neither of these features will provide a compelling reason for a widespread 802.11ac deployment. In that case, it still offers the highest available capacity and best support for high-density areas within your network. Table 5-2 compares the performance of the first two waves of 802.11ac.

Table 5-2. Performance comparison of 802.11ac waves

Protocol feature	First-wave gain over 802.11n	Second-wave gain over 802.11n
256-QAM data rates	1.33x	1.33x
80 MHz channels	2.1x	Same as first wave
160 MHz channels	Not available	4.3x
Up to eight spatial streams	No gain—first wave is 3 SS	1.33x—second wave is 4 SS
Multi-user MIMO	Not available	~2x?
TOTAL	**2.8x**	**~15x?**

Client Device Mix

As much as network administrators would like to believe that networks are their own reward, a network exists to get work done. The number, types, and capabilities of devices attached to the network are an important part of the planning process. One set of data for input into the planning process would be information on the existing devices attached to your wireless LAN today, and your existing wireless network management system should report the client mix in a variety of ways. However, in building a network, it is important to look ahead over the life of the network. In 2013, for example, only a few client devices will be 802.11ac-capable, but within a year 802.11ac will be widely available in client devices. Previous physical layers for wireless LANs have followed similar adoption trajectories. At first, the new technology is used in high-density and high-capacity areas; as those areas take hold, they support enough of a volume increase to drive down the cost of the new technology for everybody.

Table 5-3 shows the evolution of client capabilities as they move from 802.11n to the first wave of 802.11ac technology. Naturally, there will be departures from the table, but the general rule is that high-end laptops will use the fastest connectivity available while small battery-powered devices will use power-efficient single-stream interfaces. Low-end laptops fall somewhere in between and will typically settle for a less expensive wireless interface that has middle-of-the road capabilities. High-end tablets may also opt for two-stream interfaces.

Table 5-3. Effect of 802.11ac on client capabilities

Type of device	Radio type (in 2013 & earlier)	Channel width (2013 & earlier)	Data rate (2013 & earlier)	Radio type (2014)	Channel width (2014)	Data rate (2014)
Dual-band smartphone	802.11n, 1-stream	20 MHz	72 Mbps	802.11ac, 1-stream	20/40/80 MHz	Up to 433 Mbps
VoIP handset	802.11a/b/g or 1-stream 802.11n	20 MHz	54 Mbps	802.11a/b/g or 1-stream 802.11n/ac	20 MHz	Up to 87 Mbps

Type of device	Radio type (in 2013 & earlier)	Channel width (2013 & earlier)	Data rate (2013 & earlier)	Radio type (2014)	Channel width (2014)	Data rate (2014)
Tablet	802.11n, 1-stream	20/40 MHz	72 or 150 Mbps	802.11ac, 1-stream	20/40/80 MHz	Up to 433 Mbps
Netbook/low-end laptop	802.11n, 2-stream	40 MHz	Up to 300 Mbps	802.11ac, 2-stream	80 MHz	867 Mbps
High-end laptop	802.11n, 3-stream	40 MHz	Up to 450 Mbps	802.11ac, 3-stream	80 MHz	1.3 Gbps

Although 802.11ac is often dismissed as too power-hungry for mobile devices, single-stream 802.11 MIMO devices do not require significantly more power than their SISO predecessors. The main consumer of power in a MIMO device is the power-hungry digital signal processor that performs spatial mapping. By using only a single spatial stream, a portable device can reap significant benefits from 802.11ac's increased speed and wider channels without paying a significant power-consumption penalty. Although there will be an increase in power requirements to use wider channels, the trade-off is that transmissions go so much faster that the analog section is on for much less time. With a net battery life benefit, 802.11ac will be adopted widely in portable devices. In fact, 2013 saw the first introduction of an 802.11ac-capable smartphone.

Information on your device mix can be gathered from several sources. Naturally, knowledge of what has been purchased is an important source of information, but with the trend away from supporting exclusively corporate-owned devices, there is a need to gather information on all of the devices using the network. One constraint on the adoption of 802.11ac is that it is supported only in the 5 GHz band, and a significant number of devices must be ready to move to the 5 GHz band to see strong benefits from 802.11ac.

 Because 802.11ac is only available in the 5 GHz band, the benefits available depend on the number of 5 GHz–capable devices on the network.

One welcome development of 802.11ac is that it is driving increased use of the 5 GHz band. Many high-end client devices have begun to support 5 GHz operation with dual-band 802.11n interfaces, and these devices reward their users with improved connectivity. Use of the 5 GHz band has been restricted to high-end devices, in large part because it is still possible to be an "802.11n" device while supporting only one band. In order to label a device as "802.11ac," it will be necessary for that device to support the 5 GHz band, even though it is almost certain that a device labeled as "802.11ac" will also support 802.11n operation in the 2.4 GHz band.

Supporting client devices in the 5 GHz band requires a somewhat denser network deployment. If you have designed your network around the needs of coverage for the 2.4 GHz band, successfully moving to 802.11ac will require more APs.

Single-Stream Devices in 802.11ac

802.11ac offers significant benefits to single-stream devices. By extending the channel width up to 80 MHz, it makes substantial speed increases possible for single-stream devices, especially when there is sufficient uncongested spectrum available to transmit with wide channels. Looking forward to the next wave, multi-user MIMO has the potential to add significant performance to networks as well by transmitting to multiple single-stream clients at the same time. Unlike with 802.11n, there is no need to discount the gains of 802.11ac simply because of the presence of a significant number of single-stream client devices on the network. Even the first wave of 802.11ac APs will offer benefits to pre-11ac single-stream devices. As new generations of radio chips are produced, the performance will continue to improve, especially when MU-MIMO is available so multiple single-stream 802.11ac devices can receive transmissions simultaneously.

Application Planning

To be successful, the network must support the key applications that are in use. Many access points now offer some form of application visibility to augment your suppositions about the applications commonly used on the network, and can report on the throughput used by common applications. As an alternative to running application reporting on your network, Table 5-4 has a list of some of the most common applications that network administrators need to consider, along with the Wi-Fi Multimedia (WMM) access category that each application is typically assigned. WMM allows administrators to place traffic into four categories, with the higher-level categories receiving preferential access to the medium. In declining order of priority, traffic can be placed into queues for voice, video, best effort, or background traffic.

Table 5-4. Application throughput needs

Application	Recommended bit rate (Mbps, unless noted)	WMM access category
VoIP – voice transport	27 – 93 kbps (codec dependent)	Voice
VoIP – signaling (typically SIP)	5 kbps	Best effort
Remote display	150 kbps (without video), 1.8 Mbps (with video)	Video
Web conferencing	384 kbps – 1 Mbps	Video
FaceTime	0.9	Video
AppleTV video streaming	2.5 – 8	Video
High-definition video (compressed)	2 – 5	Video

Application	Recommended bit rate (Mbps, unless noted)	WMM access category
High-definition video (uncompressed)	20	Video
High-definition video (uncompressed HDMI)	3.3 Gbps	Video
Standard-definition video	1 – 1.5	Video
Email/web browsing	0.5 – 1.0	Best effort
File sharing	5	Best effort
YouTube	0.9	Best effort
Network backup	Available capacity	Background

The applications in Table 5-4 are all based on unicast data. In many cases, 802.11 access points will convert multicast frames to unicast frames, and the same estimation technique can be used for multicast applications.

Application throughput requirements can be used to create a rough guide for the capacity requirements of an access point. None of the applications in Table 5-4 is the classic "killer app" that absolutely requires 802.11ac, but the increased use of video distribution highlights the more limited capacity of 802.11n. The easiest way to use application throughput requirements to estimate capacity requirements is to divide the total capacity of a device by the application's bit rate; this will give you a rough estimate of the capacity needed. Although an 802.11ac AP may be capable of nearly 1 Gbps of throughput, a single-stream tablet will be unable to use all of that capacity. For example, if a single-stream device is capable of 25 Mbps of TCP throughput, it will require approximately 4% of the available airtime of an access point to do standard emailing/web browsing (1 Mbps for the application divided by the 25 Mbps capacity). A dual-radio AP could support approximately 50 such devices running the application. For 802.11ac, there may be different capabilities in the 2.4 GHz 802.11n radio and the 5 GHz 802.11ac radio, provided the target devices can use at least some of the advanced 802.11ac protocol features.

Admission control

If a significant fraction of the anticipated traffic is in the high-priority voice and video queues, part of your equipment evaluation should be about whether *admission control* is a valuable addition to your network. When admission control is enabled, client devices must request access to high-priority queues. For example, before placing a voice call, a client must send a request to the AP to reserve capacity for a VoIP data stream. The AP can then determine whether there is sufficient airtime available to accept the device, and either reserve the capacity or reject the request to connect due to insufficient airtime. Admission control is available using a feature of the 802.11 protocol called the *Traffic Specification* (TSPEC), and products supporting this capability can be certified for *Wi-Fi Multimedia Admission Control* (WMM-AC) by the Wi-Fi Alliance interoperability certification program.

Physical Network Connections

As part of building an 802.11ac wireless edge, it is necessary to connect APs to the edge of the existing network. This involves two main tasks: physically connecting the AP to the edge of the network to provide data transport services to it, and providing sufficient power to start up the AP.

Backbone connectivity

Physical connections of 802.11ac devices to the backbone are a snap. APs work as bridges and connect to existing Ethernet backbones, so any existing Ethernet can readily be extended with 802.11. Even basic two-stream 802.11ac devices can easily push more than 100 Mbps, so a gigabit backbone is a practical requirement for an 802.11ac access layer. Although some products will support bonding of multiple links, Fast Ethernet just isn't fast enough to support 802.11ac. Upgrade your network edge to gigabit speed before installing 802.11ac.

Although 802.11ac is often described as "gigabit wireless," a gigabit Ethernet connection to the AP is sufficient for the first wave of 802.11ac products. 802.11 speeds are based on the data rate used to transmit the MAC frame, and do not include the effects of protocol overhead such as interframe spacing and the need to transmit PHY headers. Unlike Ethernet, 802.11 is a half-duplex medium. When an Ethernet link is described as 1 Gbps, it is capable of operating at 1 Gbps in both directions, whereas its 802.11 equivalent is capable of operating at 1 Gbps in both directions combined. Depending on network traffic, the wireless LAN may have more upstream or more downstream traffic, but the speed of the wireless LAN is the sum of the upstream and downstream directions. To make speed even more deployment-dependent, the top data rates in 802.11 are generally available only to clients with high signal-to-noise ratios, and there is a natural distribution of access speed because as devices increase in distance from the access point the speed decreases. For 802.11ac, speeds in excess of a gigabit require high-SNR links in order to use the 256-QAM modulation, and the natural spatial distribution of clients ensures that many clients will be operating at mid-range speeds.

In most networks, the protocol overhead plus the spatial distribution of client devices away from the AP will typically lead to a maximum practical throughput of about two-thirds of the headline rate. Apply that rule to a first-wave 802.11ac AP with a 1.3 Gbps radio in the 5 GHz band and a 450 Mbps 802.11n radio for the 2.4 GHz band, and the maximum practical throughput is slightly in excess of 1 Gbps. Even with atypical mixes of upstream and downstream traffic, fitting that into a single full-duplex Ethernet link is comfortable.

For the first wave of 802.11ac, make sure the Ethernet edge is giga-bit, but don't worry about upgrading to 10-gigabit Ethernet access ports.

Capacity analysis for the connection of the access layer is an important component of ensuring sufficient backbone capacity. Although gigabit connections suffice for con-necting access points in the first wave, the access layer switches themselves should have 10-gigabit uplink capacity to the core of the network to accommodate multiple 802.11ac APs. As the capacity of 802.11ac grows in successive waves, 10-gigabit uplink capacity will become even more important.

As part of planning a first-wave 802.11ac deployment, you will want to look ahead to the second wave in 2014. Cable infrastructure needs to support a wireless LAN for much longer than the lifetime of any particular generation of access points. With the second wave of 802.11ac, the speed will rise to 1.7 Gbps in 80 MHz channels and may be as high as 3.5 Gbps if 160 MHz channel support is introduced. With those speeds, a single gigabit link may no longer be sufficient.

Several options exist for supporting the increased capacity of the wireless LAN in the second wave. One is to handwave and say that gigabit connections are sufficient, much like some network administrators used Fast Ethernet to support early 802.11n APs. In many cases, the actual connection rates will be low enough that this might be viable, especially in coverage-oriented deployments.

If cable installation is required for your first-wave 802.11ac deployment, it is possible to lay the foundation for the second wave and beyond by installing two Ethernet cables to each AP location to support bonded connections. Be sure to use high-quality cables such as Category 6 or 7. The practical throughput of a 3.5 Gbps 802.11ac radio plus a 600 Mbps 802.11n radio is probably around 2.5 Gbps total at peak, but if the 160 MHz channel support is removed, the practical throughput is probably more like 1.5 Gbps, a speed well within reach of a dual bonded gigabit Ethernet connection. If you have an existing cable plant, it is likely to be expensive to return to the cable plant to add a second Ethernet link, but if the cable installation is new with the 802.11ac deployment, it's a good idea to install two cables just to be safe. The major cost of installing cable is labor, and the decision to install two cables will not add significantly to the cost.

For new cable plants to support 802.11ac, install two Ethernet ca-bles. Bonded 1-gigabit Ethernet connections are future-proof and will support the second wave of 802.11ac.

Depending on your deployment scenario, there are additional reasons to consider two ports. As wireless LANs continue their march toward being the only access method for many devices, providing a highly redundant service becomes even more important. Dual-homed access points can draw power and connect to the network core through redundant paths, which may be attractive for certain types of deployments. For example, a financial firm that conducts trading operations or a health care organization supporting patient care and monitoring over a Wi-Fi network will want to carefully guard against even brief outages.

As 802.11ac continues to evolve, even higher speeds may be required. At the time this book went to press, 10-gigabit connections were only available over fiber cables. Fiber does not support power transmission, and thus is unlikely to be offered as an AP connection technology. There are efforts underway to supply power over 10 gigabit copper connections, but at the time this book was written, even 10-gigabit switches with copper connections were not very common.

Power requirements

The electrical power requirements of 802.11ac will be higher than for previous 802.11 standards. Although 802.11ac radio chips are more efficient than prior chips, they are doing significantly more work. Additional spatial streams and wider channels require more sophisticated signal processing, so gains in power efficiency are outweighed by the new protocol capabilities. With higher data rates, frames are shorter and there is a significantly higher frame rate. All this adds up to higher resource requirements at the AP: more power for new radios, more buffer memory for frame operations, and higher-powered CPUs to do more to each packet at higher frame rates. As a result, 802.11ac APs are unable to work within the 13-watt budget of 802.3af.[1]

 802.11ac APs will not offer full functionality with 802.3af, so part of the planning process should be to identify how to provide the required power to new APs.

Power options for 802.11ac are basically unchanged from previous generation of wireless LAN access points. The easiest way to provide additional power to run 802.11ac APs is to provide power using 802.3at (sometimes called "PoE plus"), a newer power standard that provides up to 25.5 watts at the end of a full-length Ethernet cable. 802.3at

---

1. Many 802.3af power injectors are able to supply substantially more power than the specification requires, through a combination of high-quality components, shorter-than-maximum-length cable runs, and high-quality cabling. Even taken together, though, these sources of headroom are only good for a few watts. The increased resources demanded by 802.11ac require more than just a few watts, so headroom won't save you from a power upgrade.

power is provided by many newer edge switches and can be added onto existing networks by using mid-span power injectors.

Alternatively, APs can be powered by DC power adapters if there are outlets readily available at the installation locations. If power outlets are unavailable, it will probably be quite expensive to add them to the best locations for AP installation, which are typically in the ceiling. Some products have the ability to draw power simultaneously from multiple power over Ethernet (PoE) connections, which enables these products to add two 13-watt 802.3af sources together for higher power draw. In most cases, the cost of running a second cable to existing AP mounting locations is prohibitive compared with that of purchasing mid-span injectors.

Security

802.11ac does not make fundamental changes to the 802.11 security architecture, nor does it introduce new features that require significant changes in your existing network security systems. Any network security devices in place for an existing wireless LAN will continue to work after an upgrade to 802.11ac unless they need to access the wireless medium directly. The biggest change to network security in 802.11ac might be based on the equipment you choose to use for 802.11ac—i.e., you might want to install equipment that offers new per-user capabilities that your previous network equipment did not.

Link-layer encryption

802.11ac does not support the use of anything other than AES-based encryption (CCMP and GCMP) to protect data frames.[2] To take advantage of the fast data rates in 802.11ac, you will have to retire any TKIP-based networks. Many 802.11ac devices will continue to support TKIP for client operations, but when doing so will limit transmission rates to pre-802.11ac data rates. To lift the cap on network capacity, you will need to convert the network over to a new encryption method.

> Many 802.11ac devices will support TKIP, but will only do so with older performance-limiting 802.11a/b/g rates.

One method of transitioning away from TKIP is to run parallel networks on the same infrastructure by duplicating an existing TKIP network on newer APs. By monitoring the usage of the TKIP network, it is possible to determine when enough older devices

---

2. CCMP is sometimes used interchangeably with the name of the Wi-Fi Alliance certification program that tests for CCMP interoperability: Wi-Fi Protected Access, version 2 (WPA2).

have been retired and the TKIP-compatible network may be decommissioned. As an alternative to parallel networks, both encryption protocols can be run simultaneously on the same SSID, which is sometimes called *mixed-mode operation*. In a mixed-mode network, the encryption method must be supported by all clients—in this case, this means the lowest common security denominator of TKIP will be used, which will limit performance, especially for applications that make extensive use of broadcast and multicast traffic.

Fast roaming

Real-time applications such as voice and videoconferencing require uninterrupted access to the radio medium, even when moving between APs. Therefore, the ability to move connections rapidly between APs is critical for real-time applications such as voice and videoconferencing. When security must be included as part of the handoff between APs, there are two major implementation paths. Opportunistic Key Caching (OKC) moves the master key between APs and is widely available in network equipment. The 802.11r specification also provides a guaranteed fast transition capability and is the foundation of the Wi-Fi Alliance's Voice-Enterprise certification program.

Management frame protection

In 2009, the 802.11 working group ratified 802.11w, a standard for the protection of management frames. Unicast management frames are protected with CCMP and encrypted to prevent eavesdropping, while broadcast management frames are authenticated with the Broadcast/Multicast Integrity Protocol (BIP). 802.11ac has no mandates regarding management frame protection, but it is likely that the initial 802.11ac products will be some of the first available products with management frame protection. Therefore, you should consider whether to use management frame protection on your network. Management frame protection can be operated in one of two modes:

Management frame protection capable
> In this mode, an AP will advertise that it can protect management frames. If a client that supports management frame protection attaches to the network, the AP will encrypt management traffic to it.

Management frame protection required
> In this mode, an AP advertises not only that it can protect management frames, but also that clients must support the capability to use the network. If a client is unable to support management frame protection, it will not be allowed to connect to the network.

Management frame protection is potentially a worthwhile capability if you are using devices that make extensive use of management frames, such as devices that support the Wi-Fi Alliance's Voice-Enterprise certification.

Authentication

802.11ac made no changes to the 802.1X authentication framework. Any user authentication system that works with 802.11a/b/g/n networks will also work with an 802.11ac network.[3] EAP-based authentication is designed to work on top of many different physical layers, and therefore it does not require any changes when moving to 802.11ac. Connections between the wireless network and the user account system should not need to be redesigned.

Additional Planning Considerations

Wireless networks do not have many vendor-independent management tools and protocols. An important part of planning a network and evaluating equipment is to assess the vendor management tools that are typically tightly integrated with the APs. Management tools typically perform both configuration management and ongoing monitoring.

To develop a way of assessing products, it will help to devise usage scenarios for what the network must support. Almost universally, a wireless network needs to support employee access as well as guest access. Commonly, employee access will be differentiated in some fashion, such as by user role or device type. Contractors and consultants may be given even more restricted access.

Guest management

Wireless networks are so useful that they often are key infrastructure for additional services offered by the IT team. One of the most notable examples is guest services, which may be composed of guest registration, authentication, and billing, or some subset of the three. Now that mobile devices almost universally use wireless LANs to access the network, wireless LAN deployments are often used to provide guest access to visitors. An adjunct to many wireless LAN deployments is a guest management system that is used to manage accounts for visitors.

Guest management systems have recently taken on a related role as a differentiator between corporate-owned devices and employee-owned devices. Enthusiasm for bring-your-own-device (BYOD) programs is based on the productivity increases that flow from putting information quite literally in the hands of users. Designing a technical architecture for a BYOD program is a book topic in itself; one of the core technical problems that must be solved is finding a way to distinguish corporate-owned devices from employee- or visitor-owned devices so that different policies can be applied to these sets of devices. In addition to flexible security models and policies, a BYOD

---

3. See Chapter 22 in *802.11 Wireless Networks: The Definitive Guide* for a detailed discussion of building a user authentication system for your wireless LAN.

program may require building a network that requires a significantly higher level of service due to increases in device density.

Intrusion detection

Wireless intrusion detection systems were once considered a standard part of the network administrator's toolkit, due to the relatively weak security mechanisms available to wireless LAN devices in the era before 2003. The improved cryptographic capabilities available for both data protection and management frame security have mitigated known attacks, and most wireless LAN system vendors have moved to integrate containment capabilities into their product lines by controlling the wired network.

802.11ac Radio Planning

With planning complete, it's time to pick out equipment to build the network. Developing solid requirements, as outlined in the previous section, is an important step in understanding what the network needs to do. Many of those requirements can be translated into a tentative plan that helps guide selection of hardware. Good project management practices are somewhat iterative. Begin with a rough estimate of your network requirements, and short-list vendors that can help meet your requirements. Bring in demonstration equipment to prove out the basic design, and gather information to refine your rough estimate. Above all, don't be afraid to put some load on your network as you are proving the concepts.

Available Radio Channels

802.11ac uses the 5 GHz spectrum exclusively, and at the time this book went to press, it had 22 available 20 MHz channels for use. In deployment practice, 14 of those channels require the use of Dynamic Frequency Selection (DFS) to protect radar operations. At an 80 MHz channel width, however, the number of available channels shrinks to just five, and three of those five channels require DFS support. Although the number of channels is reduced substantially, five channels is still sufficient to provide channel separation in almost any area that will see a wireless LAN deployment. Once the proposed spectrum expansion described in Chapter 2 is finalized, four more 80 MHz channels will be added.

Coverage and Capacity Estimates

An important step in the planning process is to estimate the number and type of APs that you will need to build your network. The AP count can be estimated for a network that provides basic coverage, or it can be estimated based on the capacity or transaction requirements identified for the network. Both types of estimates are important, especially for dense networks that have significant numbers of hot spots with high user density. "Coverage-oriented" networks provide basic connectivity for a low density of devices and can be built successfully without advanced features. Increasingly, however, networks are being built around capacity, and 802.11ac is the core technology that will enable the next generation of "capacity-oriented" networks. If you are not building a network around high capacity, you probably do not need 802.11ac. Table 5-5 is a basic comparison of the two approaches to building a network.

Table 5-5. Network characteristics

Attribute	Low-density network	High-density network
Number of clients supported per AP	Low	High
Typical distance between APs	Higher	Lower
Floor area covered by an AP	5,000 square feet (500 square meters) or more	2,000–3,000 square feet (200–300 square meters)
802.11 physical layer type	802.11n	802.11ac
Typical signal strength and signal-to-noise ratio in AP handoff area	−80 dBm (about 20 dB SNR)	−67 dBm or higher (about 33 dB SNR)
Radio design	Optimized for area of coverage	Optimized for throughput per unit of coverage area
Target frequency band	2.4 GHz (sometimes 5 GHz)	5 GHz
Load balancing/band steering	Not needed due to common lack of dual-band client devices	Required
Quality of service	Not needed	Required
Application mix	Light usage of best effort data	Voice and/or video are present

Even within a single network, both approaches may be used depending on the area. When planning out a network, designers will need to mix the two approaches to make it successful. Stairwells and hallways are often areas where users need connectivity while in transit, but the user density and application demands of the typical stairwell are quite small compared to those of conference rooms, auditoriums, and office space. In such sparsely used areas, it is acceptable to design for lower capacity and a more moderate signal quality, perhaps even using less expensive 802.11n access points.

Turning the raw data of network devices and applications into a running network requires combining the data on network goals with your knowledge of the physical space. To do so, run through a checklist like the following:

1. Get plans for the area the wireless LAN needs to cover. Many buildings have blueprints available as computer-aided drafting (CAD) files, but CAD-based processing is overkill in most cases. When you get the building plans, make sure that either they are to scale, or the planning tool you are using allows scaling of the drawings. For drawings that do not have a scale, it is possible to get a rough scale by labeling a doorway as 3 feet (1 meter) wide, or by taking the external dimensions of the building.

2. Divide up the physical space into areas of differing capacity based on your judgment of expected usage of the network. In corporate environments, areas where high capacity should drive the layout include conference rooms, offices, and cubicles. In educational settings, capacity drivers include classrooms and lecture halls. In hospitals, areas where wireless LANs support critical care drive capacity, especially when used with high-capacity applications like imaging. Be sure to account for the types of clients in use in each area, and include plans for growth. As your clients transition from one- and two-stream 802.11n clients to 802.11ac clients, the demands on the network will grow.

 If you're expecting to support significant usage, be sure to have usage estimates to match. Do not be afraid of building too much coverage at this point—it is usually harder to expand a network than to cut it back.

3. Estimate your capacity and coverage needs. For each capacity area in your plan, the estimate requires multiple calculations. When planning networks, I use several metrics to come up with an AP count and draw upon my own experience in blending them or choosing between them. Most importantly, for a high-capacity area, ensure that the 5 GHz band coverage is sufficient. For maximum throughput, neighboring APs should not be located on the same channel and should be located as far as possible from adjacent channels.[4] 802.11ac is only supported in the 5 GHz band in large part because of these advantages. To estimate 5 GHz coverage, you can use a planning toolset to design coverage with at least a 30 dB SNR. Or, if you know you know the noise floor within your environment, you can design the coverage around a signal strength based on that SNR. In some cases, the manufacturers of devices that you are targeting for support can supply design criteria. Many voice device vendors, for example, will suggest that a network be designed around a signal strength of –67 dBm.

Another estimate of capacity is based on rough back-of-the-envelope calculations of airtime. As described in "Application Planning" on page 93, you can get an extremely rough estimate of the amount of airtime a device will need by comparing its total TCP throughput to the application requirements. With a guess at the number of clients and the airtime consumption of each, you can derive an estimate of the number of APs required.

---

4. With three channels, it is not possible to lay out a network where neighboring APs do not use adjacent channels. This constraint is one of the many reasons why the 2.4 GHz band is not a good choice for a capacity-oriented network.

For example, if there are 30 tablets in a classroom and each tablet requires 4% of the available airtime, then two radios are required.[5]

To get more precise estimates of your AP capacity requirements, more accurate test tools are available. Traffic generators can be programmed with either simulated applications or application profiles, then installed and run on test devices to simulate your deployment. In deployments with extensive tablet usage, be sure to run the traffic generator on a tablet because it is a single-stream device, often with an antenna system of average performance. Verifying performance for older physical layers (802.11a and 802.11n) may also be important for networks that need to support large numbers of older devices.

4. For each area that has been estimated separately, add together each area's AP count to come up with a total.

As a hard-won piece of practical knowledge, I have found that in most networks that support general office work and do not have special demands for high throughput, a standard dual-radio AP can cover about 3,000 square feet. The per-AP coverage area has hovered around 3,000 square feet since the days when 802.11b devices transmitting at 11 Mbps were considered state of the art. As wireless LAN capacity has increased, users have moved more applications onto the wireless LAN and begun to demand much higher quality service.

Initial 802.11ac AP mounting locations

Cabling is one of the biggest costs in placing APs, and the approach to determining where to put 802.11ac APs will depend on the extent to which there is existing cabling infrastructure available to support the network. Reusing an existing cable plant will save a substantial amount of money because the cost of labor for cabling installation can be roughly comparable to the cost of the access points themselves.

If 802.11ac is replacing an existing network based on earlier technology (802.11a/b/g/n), start by reusing existing cabling and surveying the area to measure coverage. If the signal quality is sufficient the existing mounting locations should be acceptable, although a few additional APs may be required to boost capacity in "hot spots" where the highest data rates are required. One factor to watch out for when swapping out older APs for 802.11ac APs is that if the network is very old and was designed around 2.4 GHz coverage, the shorter range of 5 GHz coverage may not be sufficient to provide the desired connectivity.

---

5. If 30 devices each require 4% of the available airtime, you will need 30 x 4% = 120% of the available airtime, or 1.2 radios. Because there is no such thing as a fractional radio, round up (or, in a spreadsheet, use the "ceiling" function).

APs are cheap, and staff time is expensive. Usually, it will be more cost-effective to replace existing APs in their current locations and add further capacity if necessary than to take the time to deliberately re-survey a location for a new 802.11 standard.

If, on the other hand, you are building a wireless network for the first time, the initial mounting locations should be computed with some form of planning software. Many product vendors will assist in the determination of AP locations as part of a project bid process, often by using wireless LAN planning tools. If you use software to perform a "virtual" site survey, keep in mind that there is no substitute for performing either a manual survey with an AP powered on and measured manually by a target client device, or a rigorous post-deployment survey to validate the estimates produced by the planning software. When using software tools, keep in mind that many basic tools lack the ability to specify user or device density, so be ready to modify the results of a simulated site survey to adjust them to your environmental expectations. For example, some tools will attempt to provide high-quality coverage throughout a designated coverage area, and it is up to you to move coverage from sparsely used areas such as hallways and stairwells into the real target usage areas, such as conference rooms and classrooms.

An upgrade to 802.11ac is also an ideal time to add capacity if needed. One of the ways in which 802.11ac increases speed is the new 256-QAM modulation, but 256-QAM requires high signal-to-noise ratios. 256-QAM will not work through a wall, so if one of the objectives of your deployment is to increase the peak throughput available, it may be necessary to consider putting APs within line of sight of every place that clients may gather. Planning tools can often estimate the effects of installing additional APs for capacity purposes, and may help with setting transmit power levels.

5 GHz coverage and 802.11ac-only APs

802.11ac accentuates the difference in radio range between the 2.4 GHz band and the 5 GHz band. A good rule of thumb is that the range of a radio is inversely proportional to the square of its operating frequency.[6] Physical layers at 5 GHz will naturally have a much shorter range than at 2.4 GHz. In a network designed for 802.11ac capacity, generally the APs will be placed where they are needed for 5 GHz coverage. In a network designed for 802.11ac capacity, the network will be quite dense because of the high SNR requirements to support the 256-QAM rates (MCS 8 and 9). As a result, there are likely to be places in your network where a dual-radio device does not make sense. Figure 5-1 illustrates one example of this. Four APs are used to provide high-quality 802.11ac coverage. However, due to the longer usable range of 2.4 GHz radio signals, even when

---

6. One of the reasons why the TV white space standardization effort is exciting is that the TV spectrum was around 700 MHz, giving it a range that can be measured in kilometers instead of meters.

turning the power down, three APs are sufficient to provide coverage at 2.4 GHz. One of the APs does not need to activate its 2.4 GHz radio.

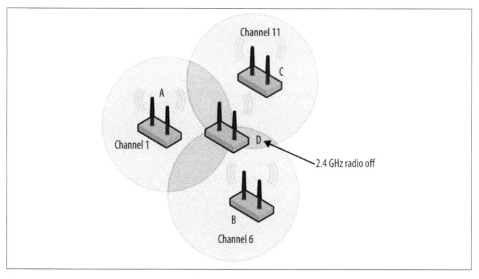

Figure 5-1. 2.4 GHz coverage completeness

A common method of adding 802.11ac capacity to an existing network is to add an 802.11ac radio to a place in space where 5 GHz coverage needs improvement. Such "infill" APs need only be 5 GHz–capable, but should come from the same vendor as the dual-radio devices already used on your network to ensure that the roaming, band steering, and load-balancing capabilities work with the rest of the network. With 802.11ac having much shorter range, the capacity-enhancing infill AP is likely going to be an increasingly large component of your network architecture. If the newly added AP has dual radios, the 2.4 GHz radio can be used as a full-time sensor. Applications for sensors are varied, but they include full-time wireless security sensors and dedicated spectrum monitors. Some vendors can use such radios as client devices to test actual performance.

Equipment Selection

With an estimate of the number of APs and their tentative initial locations, it is time to start picking out an actual implementation, rather than working with generic APs. At a high level, APs connect the free-flowing wireless world with the high-performance, fixed-in-place wired world. After reviewing your network requirements and determining what constraints drive the logical architecture, it's time to pick out your access point hardware. Access points all perform the same basic function in that they shuttle frames between radio networks and Ethernet LANs, but there can be tremendous differences in cost and functionality. Comparing access points on the basis of price alone may prevent you from discovering a critical feature that improves your ability to manage and run the network. If you're building a network of more than just a handful of access points, you probably want to look beyond the hardware available at electronics stores and at highly functional APs. Here are some things you may want to consider:

Wi-Fi Alliance interoperability certification

In June 2013, the Wi-Fi Alliance launched an interoperability program for 802.11ac. Ensuring that your product vendor has successfully passed interoperability testing is not an absolute guarantee of interoperability, but it is a strong statement that the manufacturer believes in interoperability and has taken steps to ensure compatibility with a wide variety of client devices. To check on the certification status of a product, visit the Wi-Fi Alliance website (*http://www.wi-fi.org/*) and click on the "Wi-Fi CERTIFIED Products" button on the lefthand side of the page.

High performance

Performance is not just a matter of the rate at which products push data. Many products are capable of pushing "air rate" data speeds, but only corporate-grade APs have "air rate" performance while providing a sophisticated feature set under heavy load. As with many other areas of networking technology, vendors of corporate-grade hardware invest much more heavily in software tuning because their products are used in deployments where more than just the number of bits per second matters. This investment pays dividends in providing high data rates at longer ranges from the AP with higher numbers of active client devices.

Hardware quality and robustness

Corporate-grade devices are designed to be used for many years before replacement, and therefore are often designed with future expandability in mind. Components are selected with a view toward quality and long life, instead of basing decisions primarily on cost. Sophisticated antennas or other radio frontend components may be used to improve the quality of the network, either in terms of throughput or coverage. Radios will be enabled on all available channels, even though the cost of regulatory compliance before using DFS channels can be substantial, and software supports automatic configuration of radio channel selection. Some deployment areas may require specialized hardware designs due to either very high or very low operating temperatures.

Software functionality, upgradability, and quality

Generally speaking, more expensive devices have significantly more functionality, with advanced features in several areas. Vendors regularly plan for the release of such features, and it is common for new features to be provided midway through a product's life cycle. Understanding the future functionality that might be delivered and whether your deployment would benefit from planned features allows you to consider new features appropriately in the decision process. Additionally, extensive

QA testing is used to ensure that corporate-grade devices can be run for months at a time under heavy loads.

Antenna options

Internal antennas allow an AP to be self-contained and to blend smoothly into the aesthetic environment. External antennas typically have higher gain, which improves range. In a deployment based on area of coverage instead of density, or a deployment in a challenging radio environment, selecting the right external antenna can make the difference between a poor-quality network and a successful one. External antennas are also frequently used for outdoor deployments. Picking the right external antenna is still something of an art, and the antenna must be matched to the performance characteristics of the AP. A high-gain antenna will dramatically increase the transmit range of an AP, but if the AP has low receive sensitivity, the high-gain antenna will cause more problems than it solves.[7] Product manufacturers are responsible for obtaining regulatory authorization for each type of external antenna used, so a larger selection of external antennas indicates more extensive regulatory testing.

Power options

Consumer-grade devices are typically powered with a "wall wart" transformer and must be installed close to existing electrical outlets, while corporate-grade devices can draw power from the device at the other end of the Ethernet cable. Power over Ethernet enables placement of devices in out-of-the way locations, and can be used to provide power even on very high ceilings.

Security

Security is not just about providing solid encryption, though that is the obvious starting point. Corporate-grade products offer flexible authentication through RADIUS and directory interfaces, per-user VLAN mapping, traffic filtering and queuing, and built-in captive web portals for web-based authentication. Fast roaming support extends the basic encryption to support mobile applications.

Quality of service

At the most basic level, quality of service support involves compliance with the Wi-Fi Multimedia (WMM) certification requirements, which divides traffic on the air into four classes of differing priority. More complex queuing systems can be used to improve service quality for voice devices, or to ensure that airtime is balanced fairly between network users.

---

7. Receive sensitivity is not commonly reported on data sheets but may be available in the FCC test reports for equipment that you are considering.

Manageability

If you are reading this book, you need centralized management. Evaluate management tools for a wireless network in the same way you evaluate management tools for a wired network. Ensure that the management software provides something beyond simple configuration management and can report on the overall state of the network.

Network Architecture for 802.11ac

Throughout the evolution of wireless LAN technology, there have been a number of approaches to adding the wireless LAN access layer onto an existing wired backbone network. Most approaches share two fundamental attributes, and they remain unchanged by 802.11ac. Fundamentally, 802.11 provides MAC-layer (or, after the OSI nomenclature, "layer 2") mobility. As an 802.11 station moves throughout the coverage area of the network, from the perspective of the routing and switching infrastructure it remains in a fixed spot. All commercially available products that support large-scale networks have extended the fundamental MAC-layer mobility to encompass the entire network, sometimes even going so far as to make a single subnet available in many different locations with VPN technology. Additionally, ever since the 2006 introduction of WPA2, the 802.1X security framework (sometimes also called "WPA2-Enterprise" after the Wi-Fi Alliance certification program) has provided strong authentication and transparent encryption to client devices. The 802.1X framework offers network administrators the capability of designing network authentication around user-specific policies, often assigning a bundle of access rights (variously called a "profile" or a "role") to users upon connection to the network.

Many network administrators are familiar with the concept of protocol layering and the Open Systems Interconnection (OSI) model. Network protocols are often classified by where they fit in the OSI model. Less well known, but just as important, is the separation of network technologies into *planes*, as shown in the depth dimension of Figure 5-2. Each plane has its own protocol layers, of course, but each plane also has a specialized purpose. Common planes include the following:

Data plane (sometimes called the "forwarding plane")

Protocols in the data plane move bits from one location to another and are concerned with moving frames from input interfaces to output interfaces. In an IP network, the main data plane protocols are TCP and IP, with applications such as HTTP riding on top of the network and transport layers.

Management plane

The management plane provides protocols that allow network administrators to configure and monitor network elements. In an IP network, SNMP is a protocol in the management plane. A vendor's configuration application would also reside in the management plane; wireless LANs may use CAPWAP as a transport protocol in the management plane. Without exception, large-scale IP networks use central-ized management and thus have a centralized management plane. The management plane of the network is responsible for planning and implementation, policy defi-nition, and ongoing monitoring.

Control plane

The control plane helps make the network operate smoothly by changing the be-havior of the data plane. An IP network uses routing protocols for control, while switched networks use the spanning tree protocol. The control plane of a wireless LAN is responsible for ensuring mobility between access points, coordinating radio channel selection, and authenticating users, among other tasks. The control plane is also responsible for enforcing policy.

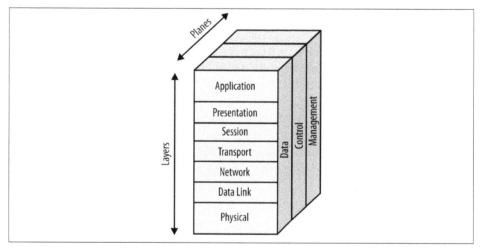

Figure 5-2. Network protocol architecture: layers and planes

Wireless networks can be classified based on the location of the control plane, and much of the development across the history of wireless LANs has been about refinements to the control plane. Early wireless LANs were built out of completely independent APs. The management plane was practically nonexistent (consisting of the APs' serial ports and, in a highly engineered network, perhaps a terminal server), and the control plane was not unified. Networks based on autonomous APs did not automatically select channels and did not always support smooth handoff between APs without proprietary protocol extensions at both ends of the link.

The development of wireless LAN controllers a decade ago led to a redesign in the way that networks were built, with the control and management planes being centralized in this new piece of the network. In a typical controller-based deployment, the access points have limited functionality without a connection to the controller. Authenticating and authorizing users is handled by the controller, as are algorithms that provide RF management functions such as channel selection. Centralized management and control made much larger networks possible, and essentially, nearly every large-scale network built prior to the emergence of 802.11n was built using a controller-based architecture. In addition to the control and management planes, early controller-based network architectures centralized the data plane as well. All data from APs was forwarded through the controller; this is often referred to as a *network overlay* because the wireless network was separate from the existing core network and existed as a layer on top of the existing core. In effect, the controller took on the role of a distribution switch for users attached to APs and provided mobility by serving as an anchor for the logical point of attachment. Early applications of wireless LANs were driven by application-specific traffic, not general-purpose user access, which made the overlay model acceptable to network administrators.

With the emergence of higher-speed wireless network technologies, there was a shift in how wireless LANs were used: rather than simply being small one-off deployments to automate processes, they became general-purpose access methods. Add-on PC cards were replaced by 802.11 interfaces integrated into the motherboard. With the standardization of 802.11n and 802.11ac traffic volumes have increased dramatically, due to both the higher speeds and the increase in the number of wireless devices attached to a typical network. As network load increased, centralized forwarding through controllers became a traffic bottleneck. Many vendors responded to the bottleneck by moving the forwarding decision out of the controller and back to the AP at the edge of the network, an approach often referred to as *distributed forwarding* because the data plane function has moved from the controller out to the AP, and, in fact, back to a parallel location with wired traffic. Although this architecture looks superficially similar to autonomous APs, it is typically paired with centralized management. Increased processing power also made varying control plane implementations possible, enabling distributed AP architectures to handle typical control functions by working among themselves.

Architecture comparison

Building a "micro-network" of an AP or two is easy. With a small number of APs, it is acceptable to manage the APs individually. Upgrading to 802.11ac is also straightforward: take out your existing 802.11a/b/g/n APs and replace them with 802.11ac APs. At such a small scale, almost anything will work. At some point, however, the overhead of managing individual devices will be too great. At this point, you are building a small- or medium-sized network. These networks have just as much to gain from 802.11ac.

Prior to the introduction of distributed APs, most networks needed a centralized control plane to handle the loads imposed by large numbers of users, and the choice between autonomous APs and controller-based APs was a straightforward one that was almost always resolved in favor of the more advanced centralized control plane. With the explosion of 802.11 devices now available, network architects have designed higher and higher capacity networks, stressing the centralized control plane. Early controller-based networks were able to use a single controller as the focal point for both the control and the data plane, but that assumption no longer holds.

Table 5-6 compares the three basic types of APs described in this section. In reality, there is some overlap between these architectures when they are implemented in products. It is likely that a large-scale network at any speed—especially one supporting critical applications—will require some degree of decentralization, either by moving some of the data plane functions to the edge of the network, moving some of the control plane functions to the edge of the network, or both. All three architectures are capable of supporting any set of network requirements, but the cost and availability of the resulting network may vary.

Table 5-6. Architecture comparison

Attribute	Autonomous APs	Controller-based APs	Distributed APs
Location of data plane	Distributed, enabling high network performance.	Centralized, potentially limiting performance to the forwarding capacity of a controller. Good mobility support because devices attach through the controller.	Distributed, enabling high network performance. Many products have features to assist with mobility.
Location of management plane	Depends on product; often distributed, imposing very high staff costs.	Centralized, lowering operational expenses.	Depends on product; often centralized, enabling lower operational expenses.
Location of control plane	Distributed, if it exists. Nonexistent control plane limits flexibility of security and radio management.	Centralized, with high functionality for radio management and user management.	Distributed. Functionality of control plane depends on vendor implementation.

Selecting a network architecture

Management plane. If you are building a network consisting of more than a handful of APs, there is no consideration. Centralized management is a must, if only because maintaining consistent policy configuration across multiple devices is easier when you can change network-wide policies and apply them to devices from a central location, similar to the way that centralized management tools for wired networks allow policies to affect the configuration on many devices. Some early wireless LAN products lacked centralized management, but these were quickly replaced by products that could be used with a centralized management system. Many flavors of centralized management exist, with wide variations in functionality and cost. Even though centralized management was formerly only accessible to large-scale networks, the emergence of the software-as-a-service "rental" model may offer you the ability to use a full-featured management system at an affordable cost for a small network.

Centralized management is nonnegotiable beyond just a few access points.

Data plane. The forwarding plane of wireless networks has been the subject of significant developments over the past five years. When 802.11 first reached the market, it was comparatively slow. Using the centralized forwarding path in Figure 5-3 did not impose a significant penalty on the network because wireless LAN speeds were slow enough for the choke point to keep up. When most 802.11 packets needed nearly 200 microseconds of preamble to begin transmission, the extra latency of a trip across the network core was barely noticeable. As the speed of 802.11 has increased, though, it has become harder and harder for the centralized forwarding point to keep up.

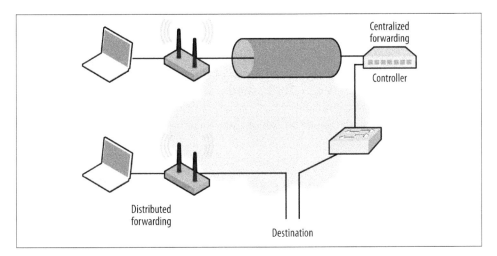

Figure 5-3. Types of forwarding paths

In practice, there is not a sharp divide between products on the market that offer a centralized forwarding path and those that offer a direct forwarding path at the access point. When controllers are used, the resulting networks may offer the choice of sending traffic either through the centralized forwarding point or directly from the AP at the network edge. As speeds have increased, the ability to offload data forwarding to the edge of the network has helped keep controllers from becoming bottlenecks on their networks. At the other end of the spectrum, APs that are generally used in distributed forwarding deployments typically offer the ability to make any VLAN accessible throughout the network by using an AP-to-AP tunnel.

The increased speeds of 802.11ac make AP-level forwarding much more attractive, especially when combined with the potential of multi-user MIMO to dramatically increase data traffic in the future.

Tunnels through the network, whether between an AP and controller or between APs, must be constructed in a way that is compatible with existing restrictions on frame size. Client devices will generally send and receive maximum-length Ethernet frames of 1,500 bytes (though they may of course use 802.11 protocol features to aggregate several of these frames together). Transporting a maximum-length Ethernet frame across an intermediate network requires either that the network support larger frames or that the tunneling protocol manage fragmentation of the client data frame plus a tunnel header.

Control plane. In a wireless LAN, the control plane maintains the logical network attachment of the client, which includes its security information, the state of any user access rights or service quality guarantees, as well as path information on how the wireless network enables data to reach the client. The control plane also manages coordination between APs for tasks such as radio management and providing network-wide quality of service. Control plane design is one of the most fertile grounds for experimentation in wireless LAN design. The location of the control plane makes an important contribution to the overall reliability and resiliency of the network. Building fully redundant wireless networks requires both resilient data forwarding and resilient control capabilities.

Most large-scale networks were originally built on centralized control plane technologies, which required that APs be in continuous contact with a control point. Many centralized control planes are now moving toward either a split control plane (where functions are shared between the controller and APs) or a more fully distributed control plane. Distributed control planes can be cheaper, especially when designing for distributed networks with many remote sites. Neither the distributed nor the centralized type of control plane is inherently more resilient; a distributed control plane protocol can be resilient by design, while a centralized control plane may require spare controllers.

Carefully evaluate the trade-offs between a centralized versus a distributed control plane from the perspectives of functionality, reliability, and cost.

Hardware Considerations

The Wi-Fi Alliance (*http://www.wi-fi.org/*) is an industry association of companies that collectively drive the development of wireless LAN technology. The Alliance is best known for the Wi-Fi CERTIFIED interoperability testing program that began in 2000. When development begins on new physical layer technologies such as 802.11ac, the Wi-Fi Alliance has a certification program to ensure that these emerging technologies are built with interoperability available from the first version. Once testing is complete and a product is awarded certification, it can be looked up at the Wi-Fi Alliance certified product listing (*http://bit.ly/11CyEE5*). Each product is also given an *interoperability certificate* that details the individual product features that have been certified.[8]

Mandatory tests

Every device submitted for 802.11ac certification must pass a series of basic tests. The features that are expected to be supported include:

5 GHz operation
> 802.11ac is a 5 GHz–only specification. All tests in the Wi-Fi Alliance certification program require operation at 5 GHz. This is in contrast to the 802.11n Wi-Fi Alliance certification program, in which 5 GHz capabilities were optional.

Channel width of 20, 40, and 80 MHz
> The initial version of the 802.11ac certification requires support of all the available channel widths up to 80 MHz. Again, this is in contrast to the Wi-Fi Alliance's 802.11n certification program, which covered only 20 MHz and 40 MHz channels (with 40 MHz channels being optional).

Dynamic bandwidth signaling
> In addition to requiring support of multiple channel widths, the 802.11ac certification test plan requires demonstrated interoperability for the dynamic bandwidth signaling protocol features described in "Dynamic Bandwidth Operation (RTS/CTS)" on page 50.

Support of MCS 0 through 7 (up to 64-QAM)
> Modulation of up to 64-QAM is required of all devices seeking 802.11ac certification.

Minimum number of spatial streams
> APs must support at least two streams before being allowed to claim 802.11ac certification; no such rule applies to client devices. There is an exception for "mobile APs," which are battery-powered devices like the Novotel Mi-Fi. Battery-powered

---

8. At the time this book was written, no 802.11ac interoperability certificates were yet available.

APs are allowed to implement only a single spatial stream. The number of tested spatial streams is likely to be placed on the interoperability certificate.

A-MPDU reception

Any Wi-Fi CERTIFIED 802.11ac device must be able to receive A-MPDU frames. A-MPDU support is typically provided within the radio chip itself, so support for this option is widespread. Devices under test are allowed to self-describe the A-MPDU size supported, so it is impossible to determine the density of back-to-back MPDUs supported.

A-MSDU reception

In addition to A-MPDU aggregation, to receive certification devices must support A-MSDU reception.

Security: TKIP & WEP negative tests

802.11ac devices may not use TKIP or WEP to protect frames sent at 802.11ac data rates. The certification program includes "negative tests," which are tests to ensure that WEP and TKIP cannot be used with 802.11ac data rates. Many products implement data rate limits when WEP or TKIP is configured, so that if an 802.11ac network is configured for TKIP, its components will avoid using data rates higher than 54 Mbps.

Optional tests

In addition to the mandatory tests described in the previous section, the certification program includes a number of optional capabilities, each of which is called out on the interoperability certificate:

MCS 8 & 9 (256-QAM support)

When the radio link has sufficient signal quality, products that implement 256-QAM can achieve throughput of 30% higher than the mandatory MCS rates.

Short guard interval at 80 MHz

Short guard intervals boost throughput by about 10%, and their use is widely supported in chipsets. An optional short guard interval test was defined for use with 802.11n, and the 802.11ac certification extends that test to the wider 80 MHz channels.

Space-time block coding (STBC)

STBC allows a signal to travel farther because it uses all of the MIMO signal processing gains to increase range. STBC was not widely implemented when it debuted with 802.11n, and remains optional with 802.11ac.

Transmission of A-MPDUs

Support for sending A-MPDUs is optional. This is the only aggregation test; the certification testing does not validate A-MSDU behavior.

LDPC
The low-density parity check adds a coding gain of about 2 dB. It is optional within the specification, but a valuable capability when used with 256-QAM to eke out as much performance as possible from the radio link.

Single-user (SU) transmit beamforming
Single-user transmit beamforming offers a potential gain of about 3–5 dB.

Modular Access Point Design

Like 802.11n before it, 802.11ac comes with a "roadmap" and several phases to be passed through before full capability is delivered. Some vendors have delivered modular radios they refer to as "future-proof" because the radio modules can be upgraded. Unfortunately, for customers the effect of modular APs is that you purchase one AP for the price of two and a half APs, and typically get substandard performance as a bonus for spending the extra money.

When building a modular AP, designers start with a chassis that accepts upgraded radios. The chassis defines the system resources available for the life of the product. (As far as I know, no modular AP has been produced with an upgradable processor card like those used in switches and routers.) Designers must build in extra CPU and memory to provide enough power to accommodate later upgrades. As a buyer, you pay for more of an AP than you need at the start to get the extra resources now. Modular APs often cost 50% more than their fixed-configuration counterparts: you pay for extra system resources now to preserve the option of upgradeability down the road.

With luck, product designers have guessed correctly at system specifications. If the future generation of hardware turns out to be more capable and resources fall short, performance will be sluggish, or the vendor will need to eliminate features and deliver a subpar product. Over the lifetime of a modular AP, the state of the art will change enough to invalidate design assumptions. An AP chassis designed before the conception of emerging features will potentially have the resources to power an 802.11ac upgrade, but it will miss out on any features that became commonplace after the chassis was designed. Modular APs suffer from the same problem as other modular products—the performance is determined by the overall system, and making just one component better rarely results in the promised performance benefit.

Another drawback is that when you go to upgrade a modular AP, there is by definition only one seller. With vendor lock-in, the cost of the upgrade module may be equivalent to the cost of a new fixed-configuration AP, designed from the ground up for current demands. Frequently, purchasers of modular APs find that by the time they are ready to change modules, newer fixed-configuration APs cost less but offer greater functionality.

All this might be worth it if modular APs saved operational costs, but they do not. Installing modules often requires more work than changing a fixed-configuration AP because the modular AP needs to be unmounted, altered, and remounted. In some cases, a new mounting bracket is needed to ensure the new antennas in the upgraded module are aligned correctly. The staff cost for adding modules is usually at least as much, and probably more than, that of just replacing APs with newer models.

Building an 802.11ac Network

Building a network may begin with detailed information gathering to make a good prediction of the number and location of APs required, or it may be more iterative, where a few APs are used to "test the waters" with a deployment in a key gathering spot for users. In iterative deployments, using the management capabilities of the wireless LAN system you are evaluating is a good way to obtain feedback on your assumptions. Is the client mix what was expected? Are the supposed key applications the most commonly used applications?

Channel Selection

At first glance, 802.11ac's addition of yet another channel width would seem to complicate the configuration process because it means network designers must manage yet another parameter with backward compatibility implications. However, the design of 802.11ac's channel coexistence mechanisms provides a rough guideline to channel allocation. Because 802.11ac clients can measure the available bandwidth, an 802.11ac network can take up as much capacity as is available, and two 802.11ac networks sharing the same frequency space can share the wide channels.

Figure 5-4 shows how a network can be built with minimum channel overlap. For the purpose of the figure, each AP's frequency space is represented by a "stack" of bars, where the shortest bar is the primary 20 MHz channel, the next-longest bar is the primary 40 MHz channel, and the longest bar is the primary 80 MHz channel. When two APs share a channel, the relevant bar is blended between two colors.

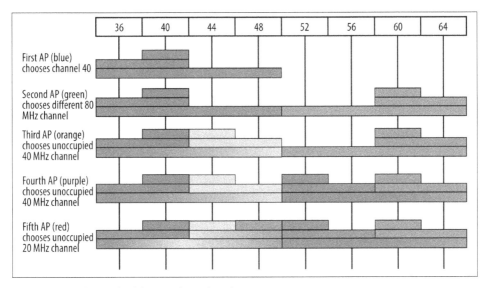

Figure 5-4. Channel addition algorithm for 802.11ac

The figure shows a network being brought up in the following steps:

1. When the first AP is powered up, it is straightforward. There is no existing network, and therefore the AP can choose any channel. In the figure, the AP represented by blue bars chooses channel 40. It will therefore take channel 40 for its 20 MHz transmissions, channels 36 and 40 for its 40 MHz transmissions, and channels 36 through 48 for its 80 MHz transmissions.

2. The second AP poses no problems, either. There is a free 80 MHz channel from channels 52 through 60, so the AP represented by green bars chooses, say, channel 60. (All four channels will choose the non-overlapping 80 MHz channel, so they are all equivalent.)

3. When the third AP, represented by orange bars, is added, it has no free 80 MHz channel. Therefore, it needs to choose a minimum-interference channel. Stepping down from the desired 80 MHz channel width, the orange AP can choose the 40 MHz channel of channels 44 and 48. The overlap between the orange and blue APs is shown by the way that the 80 MHz channel is blended between orange and blue.

4. The addition of the fourth AP, represented by purple, takes a similar path as the addition of the orange AP in the previous step. It has no free 80 MHz channel, so it must choose the least-overlapping 40 MHz channel. The only unoccupied 40 MHz channel is channels 52 and 56, so it chooses either of those two primary 20 MHz channels as its operating channel. The figure shows it choosing channel 56.

5. Finally, when the fifth AP (represented by the color red) comes up, it cannot choose an unoccupied 80 MHz channel or an unoccupied 40 MHz channel. Therefore, it

must choose a free 20 MHz channel. In the figure, it is shown occupying channel 48. The 40 MHz channel composed of channels 40 and 48 is blended between orange and red to show that it is being shared between those two APs, and the 80 MHz channel is blended between blue, orange, and red to show that all three APs share the 80 MHz channel.

This process illustrates one important advantage of 802.11ac: supporting multiple channel widths at the same time enables 802.11ac clients to "burst" capacity when it's available. Network administrators should design their networks for minimum channel overlap for wide channels, and let the narrower transmissions fall where they must to accomplish that goal. Keeping the wide 80 MHz channels as free as possible will enable as many fast transmissions as possible from 80–MHz-capable clients and is a worthy goal.

 When laying out a network, do not limit yourself to 20 MHz channels. Lay out the network using the widest channels possible and spread out the selected channels as much as possible.

Practically speaking, an extensive deployment of 40 or 80 MHz channels requires support for the worldwide harmonized radio band (channels 100 to 144 in Figure 2-3). Using these channels requires that the AP support Dynamic Frequency Selection. DFS capabilities are required by radio regulators in each individual country, and support is tested as part of the government certification process required to sell radio devices.

Network Tuning and Optimization

Part of monitoring the network is watching for conditions that will lead to substandard service, and, if possible, applying new configurations to network devices to improve performance and functionality. Fundamentally, the 802.11 MAC manages airtime. APs turn available airtime into bits sent to and from the network. Performance tuning in 802.11ac uses similar techniques to performance tuning in previous physical layers: reduce airtime contention whenever possible, and work to pack as many bits as possible into each available microsecond.

With its emphasis on technologies that assist in improving dense networks, 802.11ac APs will be packed together quite tightly. Reducing the coverage area of each AP is an important way of providing more radio capacity, but it is by no means the end of the story. Even though the 2.4 GHz band is not capable of supporting 802.11ac, it still has an important role to play as a source of capacity in busy networks. When serving areas with maximum density, enable *load-balancing* features in your wireless network equipment. Many products support multiple forms of load sharing to optimize network performance. Identifying 802.11ac clients, especially those capable of wide channel operations, and moving them to 802.11ac radios will be an important component of boosting network capacity. In high-capacity areas, multiple adjacent APs on nearby channels will need to share capacity.

Many manufacturers select default settings that are generally good for data networking and will deliver acceptable performance for web-based applications and email. In fact, many APs include a feature that gives priority to high-speed 802.11ac frames because they move data much more quickly than the older 802.11a/b/g/n frames. When transmitting a 1,500-byte Ethernet frame, 802.11ac is lightning-fast compared to its predecessors, especially if a wider channel is available for the transmission. Preferential treatment for fast 802.11ac frames has the apparent effect of speeding up the network for 802.11ac users with only minimal impact to users of older devices. The ability of a network to treat traffic differently to serve the overall user population is often called "airtime fairness" because when the throughput is optimized for the entire client population, the result is "fair."

One important performance tuning technique that is no longer available to 802.11ac network administrators is control of data rates. In 802.11a/b/g/n, it was possible for network administrators to control which data rates were supported. To avoid devices falling back to airtime-hungry low data rates, network administrators often disable low data rates. Deactivating low rates often has another second desirable side effect in that it encourages devices to move off APs with marginal connections toward better APs. However, the 802.11ac protocol does not offer control of individual data rates. Devices must support all non-256-QAM data rates, and the only control offered by the protocol in the MAC capability information element (see "The VHT Capabilities Information element" on page 40) is over the 256-QAM rates.

 Unlike 802.11n, the 802.11ac protocol does not provide the capability to control individual data rates. In 802.11n, all 76 MCS rates could be individually selected. 802.11ac uses a different method of determining data rates and has a much smaller MCS set. In 802.11ac, only three choices are available: MCS 0–7, MCS 0–8, or MCS 0–9.

Voice

In contrast to data-oriented networks, some special configuration may be helpful for networks that support extensive amounts of voice traffic. Voice traffic is demanding because it cannot be buffered, so many of the efficiency enhancements in 802.11ac are not used by voice handsets. The core of voice tuning is reducing latency for as much traffic as possible. Here are some of the techniques that can be used:

QoS configuration: enable Wi-Fi Multi-Media (WMM) and priority queuing
    WMM is a quality-of-service specification that can dramatically improve the quality of voice at the receiver. Not all vendors turn on WMM by default, or even make

voice the highest-priority traffic type. The single most important configuration change you can make to support higher-quality voice calls is to ensure that WMM is enabled. Some vendors also have an option for strict priority scheduling, which delivers frames in order to the receiver.

Enable admission control (WMM-AC)

Admission control requires voice client devices to request capacity for a call before enabling the call to be established. For example, a voice handset using G.711 could request that the AP allocate 80 kbps of capacity. The AP is then free to accept the request and reserve capacity, or reject the request due to a lack of capacity.

Enable fast roaming

Multiple techniques for fast roaming may be used, but the most common are opportunistic key caching (OKC) and 802.11r. Check with your voice client vendor to figure out which of them are supported.

Increase data rate used for Beacon frame transmission

Voice handsets are often very aggressive in roaming between APs, so tuning efforts will focus on decreasing the effective coverage area of APs and reducing large areas of coverage overlap. One of the most effective ways of limiting the effective range of an AP is to make its Beacon transmissions travel a shorter distance. While it is not possible to design a radio wave that stops at a certain distance, increasing the data rate of Beacon frames can be used to limit the effective range of the network. Typically, the Beacon rate will be set at a minimum of 24 Mbps, and sometimes even higher. (802.11a/g rates should be used because many voice handsets do not use 802.11n.)

Shorten DTIM interval

Many voice products use multicast frames for control features or push-to-talk (PTT) features. Multicast frames are held for transmission until the DTIM is transmitted.[9] Many APs will ship with a DTIM of 3, so multicast transmissions are delivered after every third Beacon. Setting the DTIM to 1 makes multicast delivery more frequent, at the cost of some battery life on handsets that need to power on after every Beacon to receive multicasts.

Reduce retry counters

Voice applications are highly sensitive to latency. 802.11 will automatically retry failed transmissions, but retransmissions take additional time. In voice transmission, frames should arrive on time or not at all. Using network capacity to retransmit frames after the target delivery time does not improve call quality, but it can delay

---

9. For more information on the operation of the DTIM, see Chapter 8 in *802.11 Wireless Networks: The Definitive Guide*.

other voice frames in the transmit queue. Somewhat counterintuitively, reducing the frame retry count can improve overall latency, and therefore voice quality.

Multicast

Multicast applications are often similar to voice applications in terms of the demands placed on the network. Multicast traffic streams are often video, and may not be easily buffered if they are real-time streams. Furthermore, multicast traffic has a lower effective quality of service than unicast traffic on a wireless LAN because multicast frames are not positively acknowledged. In a stream of unicast frames, each frame will be acknowledged and retransmitted if necessary. Multicast transmission has no such reliability mechanism within 802.11, so a stream of multicast frames may not be received and there is no protocol-level feedback mechanism to report packet loss. Here are some steps you can take to optimize multicast transmissions:

Shorten the DTIM interval

Just as with voice, many multicast applications depend on receiving data promptly. Setting the DTIM interval as low as possible improves the latency of multicast delivery.

Increase the data rate for multicast frames

By default, many products will select a low data rate, often 2 Mbps, for multicast transmissions in an effort to be backward compatible. While this is a laudable goal, and the choice of 2 Mbps was reasonable during the 802.11b-to-802.11g transition in 2004, low data rates for multicast no longer serve that goal. Unless there are critical applications running on 2 Mbps devices, or there are a large number of such old devices on the network without any upgrade path, you should increase the multicast data rate to reduce airtime contention. Many APs can automatically set the multicast data rate to the minimum data rate used for unicast frames to associated clients, or even the minimum unicast rate for clients in the multicast group. With 802.11ac, it is no longer possible to disable the low MCS rates, so the best that can be done is to disable the low data rates for previous physical layers.

Enable multicast-to-unicast conversion

Some APs implement a feature that converts a single multicast frame into a series of unicast frames. Multicast frames must be transmitted at a rate that can be decoded by all receivers and therefore is often relatively slow. Unicast frames can be transmitted much faster if the receivers are close to the AP. A series of positively acknowledged unicast frames may take approximately the same amount of airtime, but have significantly greater reliability.

Internet Group Management Protocol (IGMP) snooping
> One of the best ways to limit the load imposed by multicast traffic is to ensure that it is not forwarded on to the radio link if no clients are listening. Many APs implement IGMP snooping, and even if your APs do not, IGMP snooping can be configured on the switched network connecting the APs. IGMP snooping monitors membership in multicast groups and only forwards multicast traffic if there are listeners to the stream.

Checklist

When planning a network, use the following checklist:

Client count, density, and mix
> Gather information on the number of clients you expect to use the network, and, if possible, what their capabilities are. A good estimating rule is that an 802.11ac AP can serve around 30–60 clients with acceptable service, depending on the application. Identify peak data rates that each client will support.

Applications
> Identify the key applications that must be supported on the network. Ensure that these applications are tested during any proof-of-concept demonstration and before the final acceptance testing of the new network. Application requirements may also be used to guide the planning process by working to estimate the number of APs needed and ensuring appropriate APs to serve high-density areas.

Backbone switching
> Upgrade to gigabit Ethernet at the network edge to connect your APs, and make sure that the access layer has 10-gigabit uplinks into the core. Check whether jumbo frame support is required. 10-gigabit Ethernet will not be required for AP connections for the first wave of 802.11ac, but make sure it is part of your plans as 802.11ac develops. Any new cable runs for 802.11ac should include two cables.

Power requirements
> Supply power to the AP mounting locations. This will need to be PoE+ (802.3at) for full functionality, so either upgrade edge switches to use higher power or obtain mid-span injectors to supply sufficient power to run your chosen AP hardware.

Security planning
> 802.11ac does not support TKIP or WEP for security. If your network is not already on CCMP (WPA2), consider moving the network to use CCMP to avoid needing to reconfigure client devices for the proof of concept.

After planning the network, as you move into the design and deployment phases, use the following checklist:

Architecture
> The easy choice in architecture is that the management plane must be centralized. In most cases, a hybrid data plane that blends aspects of both a distributed data plane and centralized forwarding will be the right choice. Carefully evaluate the trade-offs for the location of the management plane based on application requirements and cost.

Hardware selection
> Select hardware that meets your requirements for performance and functionality and is certified by the Wi-Fi Alliance to ensure interoperability.

Coverage and capacity planning
> Based on the anticipated user density and application mix, come up with tentative AP mounting locations. Many tools are available to assist with this process, some of which are free. When laying out the network, pick the widest "native" channel width for 802.11ac.

Glossary

ACK

Abbreviation for "acknowledgement." ACKs are used extensively in 802.11 to provide reliable data transfers over an unreliable medium. For more details, see "Contention-Based Data Service" in Chapter 3 of *802.11 Wireless Networks: The Definitive Guide*.

See Also Block ACK, Implicit feedback.

AES

Advanced Encryption Standard. A cipher selected by the National Institute of Standards and Technology (NIST) to replace the older Data Encryption Standard (DES) in 2001 after a five-year evaluation. AES is a 128-bit block cipher that uses either 128-, 192-, or 256-bit keys. It has been widely adopted by many protocols requiring the use of a block cipher, including CCMP in 802.11, though CCMP uses only 128-bit keys. AES is specified in FIPS Publication 197.

AP

Access Point. A bridge-like device that attaches wireless 802.11 stations to a wired backbone network. For more information on the general structure of an access point, see Chapter 20 of *802.11 Wireless Networks: The Definitive Guide*.

AS

Authentication Server. The network service that validates user credentials. Usually RADIUS in 802.11 networks.

Basic Block ACK

The original block acknowledgement specification in the 802.11e amendment allowed a receiver of a group of frames to selectively acknowledge individual 802.11 fragments. Extensions in 802.11n make the protocol more efficient for use with 802.11n networks.

See Also Compressed Block ACK.

Basic service set

See BSS.

Beamforming

A method of using precise phase shifts on an antenna array that focuses the resulting transmission in a particular direction. Sending beamformed transmissions may require an exchange of control information to set up the antenna array.

Beamformee

The receiver of a beamformed transmission. The beamformee may need to transmit some packets in a beamforming setup exchange, but the main purpose of the beamforming exchange is to receive a directional transmission.

Beamformer

The sender of a beamformed transmission. The beamformer may need to receive some packets in a beamforming setup exchange, but the main purpose of such an exchange is to send a directional transmission.

Block ACK

A mechanism that allows the recipient of a series of frames to transmit one acknowledgement for the entire series. It enables selective acknowledgement of each frame in the series. By transmitting just one umbrella ACK frame, it makes substantially more efficient use of airtime than the traditional positive ACK transmitted in response to a single frame.

Block ACK Request

The Block ACK Request (BAR) frame is sent prior to a series of frames that the transmitter would like to be acknowledged. Without a block ACK request, the receiver cannot send a block ACK.

BPSK

Binary Phase Shift Keying. A modulation method that encodes bits as phase shifts. One of two phase shifts can be selected to encode a single bit.

BSS

Basic Service Set. The building block of 802.11 networks. A BSS is a set of stations that are logically associated with one another.

BSSID

Basic Service Set Identifier. A 48-bit identifier used by all stations in a BSS in frame headers.

Code rate

In the context of a forward error correcting code, the code rate describes the fraction of bits devoted to error correction, and is typically symbolized by R. For example, an R=1/2 code takes the input data stream and encodes every payload bit as two bits. Codes can be described as *conservative*, or able to correct large errors. Conversely, a code rate may be *aggressive*, meaning that error

correction capacity is being sacrificed for efficiency. The lower the code rate, the more conservative a code is; coding at R=1/2 enables more error recovery than coding at R=5/6.

Compressed Block ACK

A new block ACK extension defined by 802.11n. The "compression" referred to in the name refers to the fact that the compressed block ACK mechanism can only acknowledge nonfragmented frames. 802.11n uses such large aggregate frames that fragmentation is not commonly used, and the block ACK window can be made substantially more efficient by acknowledging at the frame level instead of the fragment level.

See Also Block ACK, Basic Block ACK.

Constellation

A set of points that describes a precise phase shift and amplitude. By transmitting a carrier wave with a given phase shift and amplitude, the sender conveys a symbol to the receiver.

CCM

Counter Mode with CBC-MAC. An authenticated block cipher mode defined in RFC 3610. It can be used with any 128-bit block cipher, but is commonly used with AES in wireless LANs for security.

CCMP

Counter Mode with CBC-MAC Protocol. 802.11i-2004 defined the use of AES with the CCM mode of operation as CCMP. It is the strongest encryption protocol available for use with wireless LANs, and the only security protocol allowed for use with 802.11n.

CRC

Cyclic Redundancy Check. A mathematical checksum that can be used to detect data corruption in transmitted frames. The CRC is a linear hash function, and should not be used for data security assurance.

CSMA

Carrier Sense Multiple Access. A "listen before talk" scheme used to mediate the access to a transmission resource. All stations are allowed to access the resource (multiple access) but are required to make sure the resource is not in use before transmitting (carrier sense).

CSMA/CA

Carrier Sense Multiple Access with Collision Avoidance. A CSMA method that tries to avoid simultaneous access (*collisions*) by deferring access to the medium. 802.11 and AppleTalk's LocalTalk are two protocols that use CSMA/CA.

CTS

Clear to Send. The frame type used to acknowledge receipt of a Request to Send and the second component used in the RTS-CTS clearing exchange used to prevent interference from hidden nodes.

DA

Destination Address. The MAC address of the station the frame should be processed by. Frequently, the destination address is the receiver address. In infrastructure networks, however, frames bridged from the wireless side to the wired side will have a destination address on the wired network and a receiver address of the wireless interface in the access point.

DBPSK

Differential Binary Phase Shift Keying. A modulation method in which bits are encoded as phase shift differences between successive symbol periods. Two phase shifts are possible for an encoding rate of one data bit per symbol.

DCF

Distributed Coordination Function. The rules for contention-based access to the wireless medium in 802.11. The DCF is based on exponentially increasing backoffs in the presence of contention as well as rules for deferring access, frame acknowledgment, and when certain types of frame exchanges or fragmentation may be required.

Delayed Block ACK

A method of transmitting a block ACK some time after the last data frame in the burst to be acknowledged has been successfully received.

DFS

Dynamic Frequency Selection. A spectrum management service required by European radio regulations (European Commission decisions 2005/513/EC and 2007/90/EC, along with ETSI EN 301 893) to avoid interfering with 5 GHz radar systems, as well as to spread power across all available channels. DFS was also key to the FCC decision to open up the harmonized frequency band in the US.

DIFS

Distributed Inter-Frame Space. The interframe space used to separate atomic exchanges in contention-based services.

See Also DCF.

DQPSK

Differential Quadrature Phase Shift Keying. A modulation method in which bits are encoded as phase shift differences between successive symbol periods. Four phase shifts are possible for an encoding rate of two data bits per symbol.

DS

Distribution System. The set of services that connect access points together. Logically composed of the wired backbone network plus the bridging functions in most commercial access points.

DSSS

Direct-Sequence Spread Spectrum. A transmission technique that spreads a signal over a wide frequency band for transmission. At the receiver, the widespread signal is correlated into a stronger signal; meanwhile, any narrowband noise is spread widely. Most of the 802.11-installed base at 2 Mbps and 11 Mbps is composed of direct-sequence interfaces.

DTIM

Delivery Traffic Indication Map. Beacon frames may contain the DTIM element, which is used to indicate that broadcast and multicast frames buffered by the access point will be delivered shortly.

EAP

Extensible Authentication Protocol. An authentication framework that is frequently used in wireless networks; it supports multiple authentication methods

ESS

Extended Service Set. A logical collection of access points all tied together. Link-layer roaming is possible throughout an ESS, provided all the stations are configured to recognize each other.

ETSI

European Telecommunications Standards Institute. ETSI is a multinational standardization body with regulatory and standardization authority over much of Europe. GSM standardization took place under the auspices of ETSI.

Explicit feedback

When used with beamforming, this refers to a beamforming method that requires frames to be sent between the two parties to a beamformed transmission. The beamformee must send frames that help the beamformer calibrate future transmissions.

FEC

Forward Error Correction. A type of code in which the transmitter takes the payload for transmission and encodes it with redundant bits to enable the receiver to correct errors. There are two main types: convolutional codes that work on arbitrary-length streams of data, and block codes that work on fixed-length blocks.

FCC

Federal Communications Commission. The regulatory agency for the United States. The FCC Rules in Title 47 of the Code of Federal Regulations govern telecommunications in the United States. Wireless LANs

must comply with Part 15 of the FCC rules, which are written specifically for RF devices.

FCS

Frame Check Sequence. A checksum appended to frames on IEEE 802 networks to detect corruption. If the receiver calculates a different FCS than the FCS in the frame, it is assumed to have been corrupted in transit and is discarded.

FIPS

Federal Information Processing Standard. Public standards used by nonmilitary agencies of the United States federal government and its contractors.

Four-way handshake

The key exchange defined in 802.11i that expands a pairwise master key into the full key hierarchy. The four-way handshake allows a supplicant and an authenticator to agree on dynamically derived encryption keys.

GCMP

Galois-Counter Mode Protocol. A combination of the well-known counter mode with Galois field multiplication for authentication. It provides similar security to CCMP with significantly higher performance.

GMK

Group Master Key. The key used by an authenticator to derive the group transient key.

GTK

Group Transient Key. Derived by combining the group master key with the group random number, the GTK is used to derive the group key hierarchy, which includes keys used to protect broadcast and multicast data.

HR/DSSS

High-Rate Direct-Sequence Spread Spectrum. The abbreviation for signals transmitted by 802.11b equipment. Although similar to the earlier 2 Mbps transmissions in many respects, advanced encoding enables a higher data rate.

HT

High Throughput. The official name of the 802.11n PHY, and a common abbreviation that is used colloquially to mean "802.11n."

IEEE

Institute of Electrical and Electronics Engineers. The professional body that has standardized the ubiquitous IEEE 802 networks.

Immediate Block ACK

A style of block ACK in which the Block ACK frame is sent immediately following the frames that it is acknowledging.

Implicit feedback

A method of beamforming where no explicit communication takes place between the beamformer and beamformee. Implicit feedback often uses the received frames themselves to estimate the required channel calibration. It does not produce as effective a steering matrix, but it does not require software support at both ends of the link.

ISM

Industrial, Scientific, and Medical. Part 15 of the FCC Rules sets aside certain frequency bands in the United States for use by unlicensed ISM equipment. The 2.4 GHz ISM band was initially set aside for microwave ovens so that home users of microwave ovens would not be required to go through the burdensome FCC licensing process simply to reheat leftover food quickly. Because it is unlicensed, though, many devices operate in the band, including 802.11 wireless LANs.

ITU

International Telecommunications Union. The successor to the Consultative Committee for International Telephony and Telegraphy (CCITT). Technically speaking, the ITU issues recommendations, not regulations or standards. However, many countries give ITU recommendations the force of law.

LDPC

Low-Density Parity Check. A block error-correction code that can optionally be used in 802.11.

LLC

Logical Link Control. An IEEE specification that allows further protocol multiplexing over Ethernet. 802.11 frames carry LLC-encapsulated data units.

MAC

Medium Access Control. The function in IEEE networks that arbitrates use of the network capacity and determines which stations are allowed to use the medium for transmission.

MCS

Modulation and Coding Set. A number that describes both the modulation and the forward error correcting code used.

MIMO

Multiple-Input/Multiple-Output. An antenna configuration that uses more than one transmission antenna and more than one receiver antenna to transmit multiple data streams. MIMO antenna configurations are often described with the shorthand "Y×Z," where Y and Z are integers, used to refer to the number of transmitter antennas and the number of receiver antennas, respectively.

MPDU

MAC Protocol Data Unit. A fancy name for frame. The MPDU does not, however, include PLCP headers.

MRC

Maximal Ratio Combining. A method of combining the signals from multiple antennas in an antenna array to boost the signal-to-noise ratio of a received frame. MRC uses the "extra" radio chains in an antenna array to provide additional information.

MSDU

MAC Service Data Unit. The data accepted by the MAC for delivery to another MAC on the network. MSDUs are composed of higher-level data only. For example, an 802.11 management frame does not contain an MSDU.

Multi-user

In 802.11ac, a multi-user transmission is a transmission that sends distinct frames for each member of a set of receivers. In 802.11ac, up to four receivers can be designated for a multi-user transmission.

MU-MIMO

Multi-User MIMO. The application of MIMO techniques to send different transmissions to multiple users simultaneously.

NAV

Network Allocation Vector. The NAV is used to implement the virtual carrier-sensing function. Stations will defer access to the medium if it is busy. For robustness, 802.11 includes two carrier-sensing functions. One is a *physical* function, which is based on energy thresholds, whether a station is decoding a legal 802.11 signal, and similar things that require a physical measurement. The second is a *virtual* carrier sense function, which is based on the NAV. Most frames include a nonzero number in the NAV field, which is used to ask all stations to politely defer from accessing the medium for a certain number of microseconds after the current frame is transmitted. Any receiving stations will process the NAV and defer access, which prevents collisions. For more detail on how the NAV is used, see "Contention-Based Data Service" in Chapter 3 of *802.11 Wireless Networks: The Definitive Guide*.

Noise floor

The level of ambient background "static" in an area. Transmissions must rise above the noise floor in order to be received. A good analogy for the noise floor is the burble of conversations within a room where a party is being held. In order to hear and understand a single voice, you have to be able to concentrate on it so you can hear it over the background level.

OBSS

Overlapping BSS. Refers to another network installed in the same physical space on the same channel, whether it is part of the same ESS or not. If two access points were installed next to each other on channel 6, each would be an OBSS of the other.

OFDM

Orthogonal Frequency Division Multiplexing. A technique that splits a wide frequency band into a number of narrow frequency bands and inverse-multiplexes data across the subchannels. 802.11a and 802.11g are based on OFDM. 802.11n uses MIMO to transmit multiple OFDM data streams.

PDU

Layers communicate with each other using protocol data units. For example, the IP protocol data unit is the familiar IP packet. IP implementations communicate with each other using IP packets.

See Also SDU.

PHY

Common IEEE abbreviation for the physical layer.

PMK

Pairwise Master Key. The root of all keying data between a supplicant and an authenticator. It may be derived from an Extensible Authentication Protocol (EAP) method during authentication, or supplied directly as a preshared key.

PPDU

PLCP Protocol Data Unit. The complete PLCP frame, including PLCP headers, MAC headers, the MAC data field, and the MAC and PLCP trailers.

protocol data unit

See PDU.

PS

Power Save. Used as a generic prefix for power-saving operations in 802.11.

PSDU

PLCP Service Data Unit. The data the PLCP is responsible for delivering. Typically it will be one frame from the MAC, with headers. In 802.11, however, the PSDU may consist of an aggregate of several MAC service data units.

PSK

Pre-Shared Key. In 802.11i, this refers to an authentication method depending on a statically configured authentication key that must be distributed manually. Also called WPA-PSK.

PSMP

Power-Save Multi-Poll. A power-saving system specific to 802.11n that improves both power efficiency and airtime efficiency by scheduling transmissions to associated clients.

QAM

Quadrature Amplitude Modulation. A modulation method that varies both the amplitude and phase simultaneously to represent a symbol of several bits. 802.11n uses both 16-QAM and 64-QAM at higher transmission rates.

QPSK

Quadrature Phase Shift Keying. A modulation method that encodes bits as phase shifts. One of four phase shifts can be selected to encode two bits.

RA

Receiver Address. The MAC address of the station that will receive the frame. The RA may also be the destination address of a frame, but is not always. In infrastructure networks, for example, a frame destined for the distribution system is received by an access point.

RADIUS

Remote Authenticated Dial-In User Service. A protocol used to authenticate dial-in users that has become more widely used because of 802.1X authentication. The most common type of authentication server used in 802.1X systems.

RLAN

Radio LAN. A term used by European radio regulations to refer to any wireless network built on radio technology. Although 802.11 is the most popular, others do exist. One of the better known alternative radio network technologies is ETSI'S HIPERLAN.

RF

Radio Frequency. Used as an adjective to indicate that something pertains to the radio interface ("RF modulator," "RF energy," and so on).

RIFS

Reduced Interframe Space. A shortened frame separator that allows better use of available airtime when two HT devices are communicating with each other.

RSN

Robust Security Network. A network that uses the security methods originally defined 802.11i-2004 and does not provide any support for the use of WEP.

RSSI

Received Signal Strength Indication. This is a value reported for the strength of a frame that has been received; it acts much like a "volume" indicator for the transmission. The RSSI may be reported in many different ways, but a common method is in dBm.

RTS

Request to Send. The frame type used to begin the RTS/CTS clearing exchange. RTS frames are used when the frame that will be transmitted is larger than the RTS threshold.

SA

Source Address; as disinct from TA. The station that generated the frame. Different when the frame originates on the distribution system and goes to the wireless segment.

SDU

When a protocol layer receives data from the next highest layer, it is sending a service data unit. For example, an IP service data unit can be composed of the data in the TCP segment plus the TCP header. Protocol layers access service data units, add the appropriate header, and push them down to the next layer.

See Also PDU.

Service Data Unit

See SDU.

SIFS

Short Interframe Space. The shortest of the four interframe spaces. The SIFS is used between frames in an atomic frame exchange.

Spatial stream

MIMO techniques are sometimes called *spatial reuse* because a MIMO system will send multiple independent data streams between the transmitter and the receiver. Each data stream is called a *spatial stream* because it takes a different path through space between the transmitter and receiver. An 802.11n device may have up to four spatial streams. For any given transmission, the maximum number of spatial streams is defined by the lower number.

Single user

A single-user transmission is a frame that is sent to one recipient. Contrast with multi-user.

SSID

Service Set Identifier. A string used to identify an extended service set. Typically, the SSID is a recognizable character string for the benefit of users.

STBC

Space-Time Block Coding. A method of transmitting a single data stream across multiple antennas for additional transmission redundancy.

TA

Transmitter Address. The station that actually put the frame in the air. Often the access point in infrastructure networks.

TIM

Traffic Indication Map. A field transmitted in Beacon frames used to inform associated stations that the access point has buffered. Bits are used to indicate buffered unicast frames for each associated station as well as the presence of buffered multicast frames.

TK

Temporal Key. 802.11i key hierarchies derive a temporal key to be used for authentication protocols. The temporal key is the main input to link-layer encryption protocols such as TKIP or CCMP.

TKIP

Temporal Key Integrity Protocol. One of the improved encryption protocols in 802.11i, TKIP uses the fundamental operations of WEP with new keying and integrity check mechanisms to offer additional security. 802.11n clearly forbids the use of TKIP with 802.11n frames.

WEP

Wired Equivalent Privacy; derided as "Wiretap Equivalence Protocol'" by its critics. A standard for ciphering individual data frames. It was intended to provide minimal privacy and has succeeded in this respect. In August 2001, WEP was soundly defeated, and public code was released. WEP is not supported by 802.11n devices.

Wi-Fi

An umbrella term used to refer to wireless LANs in general, and a testament to the strength of the Wi-Fi Alliance's branding activities. "Wi-Fi" is often used interchangeably with "wireless LAN" or "802.11."

Wi-Fi Alliance

The Wi-Fi Alliance (formerly the Wireless Ethernet Compatibility Alliance) started the Wi-Fi certification program to test interoperability of 802.11 implementation.

Originally, the term was applied to devices that complied with 802.11b (11 Mbps HR/DSSS), but further programs have extended PHY interoperability testing to include 802.11a, 802.11g, 802.11n and 802.11ac, as well as security.

Wi-Fi CERTIFIED

Trademark of the Wi-Fi Alliance used to indicate that a particular device has passed an interoperability test. Once certified, a product's capabilities are published in the Wi-Fi Alliance certification database, and an interoperability certificate lists certified capabilities.

WPA and WPA2

Wi-Fi Protected Access. A security standard based on 802.11i draft 3. The Wi-Fi Alliance took 802.11i draft 3 and began certifying compliance with early TKIP implementations to accelerate adoption of 802.11 security protocols. WPA2 is based on the full ratified version of 802.11i-2004. Products certified with 802.11n are only allowed to use CCMP to encrypt high-speed 802.11n frames.

About the Author

Matthew S. Gast is the director of software product management at Aerohive Networks. He has been active within the Wi-Fi technology community, holding multiple leadership roles in industry organizations. Matthew served as the chair of the 802.11-2012 revision. Within the Wi-Fi Alliance, he leads the security task groups in their investigation of new security technologies and previously led the Wi-Fi Alliance's network management task group's investigation of certification requirements for new power-saving technologies. An avid pilot, Matthew can generally be found at (or preferably above) an airport when he is not working on Wi-Fi.

Colophon

The animal on the cover of *802.11ac: A Survival Guide* is the common European eel (*Anguilla anguilla*).

The cover image is from Johnson's *Natural History*. The cover font is Adobe ITC Garamond. The text font is Adobe Minion Pro; the heading font is Adobe Myriad Condensed; and the code font is Dalton Maag's Ubuntu Mono.

Get even more for your money.

Join the O'Reilly Community, and register the O'Reilly books you own. It's free, and you'll get:

- $4.99 ebook upgrade offer
- 40% upgrade offer on O'Reilly print books
- Membership discounts on books and events
- Free lifetime updates to ebooks and videos
- Multiple ebook formats, DRM FREE
- Participation in the O'Reilly community
- Newsletters
- Account management
- 100% Satisfaction Guarantee

Signing up is easy:

1. Go to: oreilly.com/go/register
2. Create an O'Reilly login.
3. Provide your address.
4. Register your books.

Note: English-language books only

To order books online:
oreilly.com/store

For questions about products or an order:
orders@oreilly.com

To sign up to get topic-specific email announcements and/or news about upcoming books, conferences, special offers, and new technologies:
elists@oreilly.com

For technical questions about book content:
booktech@oreilly.com

To submit new book proposals to our editors:
proposals@oreilly.com

O'Reilly books are available in multiple DRM-free ebook formats. For more information:
oreilly.com/ebooks

Milton Keynes UK
Ingram Content Group UK Ltd.
UKHW052217220924
448641UK00008B/265